D0098652

When I Left Home

When I Left Home

MY STORY

BUDDY GUY

with David Ritz

Da Capo Press
A MEMBER OF THE PERSEUS BOOKS GROUP

 Printed in the United States of America. For information, address Da Capo Press, 44 Farnsworth Street, 3rd Floor, Boston, MA 02210.

Designed by Timm Bryson
Set in 13 point Vendetta Medium by the Perseus Books Group

Library of Congress Cataloging-in-Publication Data

Guy, Buddy.
When I left home : my story / Buddy Guy with David Ritz.—1st Da Capo Press ed.
p. cm.
Includes index.
ISBN 978-0-306-81957-5 (hardcover : alk. paper)—ISBN 978-0-306-82107-3 (e-book) 1. Guy, Buddy. 2.
Blues musicians—United States—Biography. 3. Guitarists—United States—Biography. I. Ritz, David. II.
Title.
ML419.G86A3 2012
787.87'1643092—dc23
[B]

2011040308

First Da Capo Press edition 2012

Published by Da Capo Press
A Member of the Perseus Books Group
www.dacapopress.com

Da Capo Press books are available at special discounts for bulk purchases in the U.S. by corporations, institutions, and other organizations. For more information, please contact the Special Markets Department at the Perseus Books Group, 2300 Chestnut Street, Suite 200, Philadelphia, PA 19103, or call (800) 810-4145, ext. 5000, or e-mail special.markets@perseusbooks.com.

10 9 8 7 6 5 4 3

In memory of Muddy, father to us all

Contents

After I Left Home

Preface

I get up at break of dawn. Been doing that my whole life. That's what happens when you grow up on the farm. Circumstances might change, but if you a country boy like me, you still hear the rooster.

My house is way on the outskirts of town in the far suburbs of Chicago on fourteen acres of land. Looking out the backyard I see trees everywhere. Got a thing for trees. I like watching how the leaves turn color in the fall, how winter frosts over the branches, how little buds break out in spring and new leaves come to life in summer. The seasons got a rhythm that connects me to the earth.

First thing on my mind are beans. Thinking about going to the store to buy beans. If I find some freshly shelled beans, I'll jump over the counter to get 'em. Get to the supermarket when the doors first open. Someone might recognize me, might say, "Buddy, what you doing here?" I say, "Hey, man, I gotta eat like everyone else. Gotta get me some fresh beans."

When the weather's warm, I want melon. But you can't sell me melon without seeds. Just like you can't sell me white-and-yellow corn. I don't fool with no food that's messed over by man. On the way home, if I see a stand on the side of the road, I'll stop to see what they got. If they got corn and I spot a little worm crawling over the top, I'll buy it. That means the corn hasn't been sprayed with chemicals. It's easy to clean out the worm, but how you gonna clean out the chemicals?

I'll spend the rest of the day in the kitchen. Maybe I'll cook up a gumbo with fresh crayfish. When I was a boy, crayfish tail was bait. Now it's a delicacy. The rice, the spice, the greens, the beans—when I get to cooking, when the pots get to boiling and the odors go floating all over the house, my mind rests easy. My mind is mighty happy. My mind goes back to my uncle, who made his money on the Mississippi River down in Louisiana where we was raised. My uncle caught the catfish and brought it home to Mama. That fish was so clean and fresh, we didn't need to skin it. Mama would just wash it with hot water before frying it up. I can still hear the sound of the sizzle. And when I bit into that crispy, crackling skin and tasted the pure white of the sweet fish meat, I was one happy little boy.

That's the kind of food I'm looking for. I'm looking today, and I'm looking tomorrow, and I'll be looking for the rest of my life.

My life is pretty simple. If I'm off the road and not getting ready to go off to New York or New Delhi, I'll spend my day shopping and cooking. Maybe the kids will come over. Maybe I'll eat alone. At 2 p.m. I'll take me a good long nap. After dinner I'll get in my SUV and see that I've put some 200,000 miles on the thing. If it's low on gas, I'll take the time to drive over to Indiana where gas is a couple of cents cheaper. I'll remember that one of my first jobs off the farm was in Baton Rouge pumping gas. Back then the average sale was $1. Today it'll cost me $120 to fill the tank. Ain't complaining—just saying I've seen some changes in these many years I've been running this race.

Around 7:30 I'll head into Chicago. My club, Legends, sits on the corner of Wabash and Balbo, right across from the huge

Hilton Hotel on the south end of the Loop. It's a big club that can hold up to five hundred people, and I'm pleased to say that I own the building that houses it.

I go in and take a seat on a stool in the back. I say hello to the men and women who work there. Two of my daughters run the place, and they're usually upstairs going over the books. Occasionally a customer will recognize me, but to most everyone I'm just a guy at the bar. That's how I like it. I don't need no attention tonight—I'm not playing, I'm just kicking back. I'm feeling good that I got a place to go at night and that Chicago still has a club where you can hear the blues. Live blues every night. Can't tell you how that warms this old man's heart.

Funny thing about the blues: you play 'em cause you got 'em. But when you play 'em, you lose 'em. If you hear 'em—if you let the music get into your soul—you also lose 'em. The blues chase the blues away. The true blues feeling is so strong that you forget everything else—even your own blues.

So tonight I'm thinking about how the blues change you and how they changed me. Thinking about how I followed the blues ever since I was a young child. Followed the blues from a plantation way out in the middle of nowhere to the knife-and-gun concrete jungle of Chicago. The blues took my life and turned it upside down. Had me going places and doing things that, when I look back, seem crazy. The blues turned me wild. They brought out something in me I didn't even know was there.

So here I am—a seventy-five-year-old man sitting on a bar stool in a blues club, trying to figure out exactly how I got here. Any way you look at it, it's a helluva story.

Before I Left Home

Flour Sack

You might be looking through a book of pictures or walking through a museum where they got photographs of people picking cotton back in the 1940s. Your eye might be drawn to a photo of a family out in the fields. There's a father with his big ol' sack filled with cotton. There's a woman next to him—maybe his wife, maybe his sister. And next to them is a boy, maybe nine years old. He got him a flour sack. That's all he can manage. After all, it's his first day picking.

That little boy could be me. I started picking at about that age. I stood next to my daddy, who showed me how to do the job right.

Depending where you coming from, you could feel sorry for that little boy, thinking he's being misused. You could feel he's too young to work like that. You could decide that the world he was born into—the world of sharecropping—was cruel and unfair. And you wouldn't be entirely wrong. Except that if that boy was me and you were able to get inside my little head, you'd find that I was happy being out there with my daddy, doing the work that the big people did. I wanted to be grown and help my family any way I could. Didn't know anything else except the land and the sky and the seasons and the fruits and the fish and the horses and the cows and the pigs and the pecans and the birds and the moss and the white cotton that we prayed came up plentiful enough to give us enough money to make it through winter.

I saw the world through the eyes of my mama and daddy. Their eyes were looking at the earth. The earth had to yield. If it did, we ate. If it didn't, we scrambled. Because we didn't have no electricity—not for the first twelve years of my life—we were cut off from what was happening outside our little spot in Louisiana called Lettsworth. I didn't know it at the time, but we were living and farming like people lived and farmed a hundred years before. When I got my little flour sack and went out in the field, I was doing something my people had been doing ever since we were herded up like cattle in Africa, sent out on slave boats, and forced to work the land of the southern states of America. That fact, though, was something that came into my mind when I was an adult playing my music in Senegal. Someone brought me to the Point of No Return, one of the places where slaves were sent off to make that terrible Atlantic crossing. Maybe that's where the blues began.

But to me—nine-year-old George Buddy Guy, son of Sam and Isabell Guy, born July 30, 1936—black history was not part of the elementary schooling I got at the True Vine Baptist Church. That's where I was taught to use utensils and read little books about white children called Dick and Jane. Black people weren't in those books. Blacks weren't part of history. All we knew was the present time. We knew today, and today meant shuck the corn and feed the pig and go to school in the evenings after our chores were done.

I had fears—snakes and lightning and ghosts who were said to haunt the graveyards. But I had something bigger than those fears—a feeling of family. Back then, family feeling was stronger than it is today. If you had a righteous mom and dad like I did, they could make you feel that, no matter what, everything was all right. If you had two older sisters like mine—Annie Mae and Fanny—and two younger brothers—Philip and Sam—who always had your back, you felt protected.

We lived in a wooden shack built up on pillars. We didn't have no indoor plumbing. When it was blistering hot and we wanted to escape the heat, we'd go under the cabin where the dirt was cool. The inside was just a couple rooms and a wood-burning stove. No running water. We pumped the water into a number-three tub for our weekly baths. We also used those tubs to soak the pecans we picked so that when we sold them by the pound, they weighed a little more.

I didn't know about glass windows. Our windows were made of wood. When it rained, we shut the windows and, if it was summertime, we sweated bullets. The crazy Louisiana weather had all kinds of storms rolling through. I once saw a killer hurricane tear the porch from the rest of our cabin and blow it some twenty feet away—with Daddy and Fanny standing right on it! When lightning ripped open the sky, I ran to Mama, who held me in her arms and whispered, "Don't say nothing, boy, that's just God doing his work."

Our work never stopped. The business broke down like this: a family owned the land and got half of everything we produced. When I was younger we lived on a smaller farm. But when I turned eight we moved to a larger plantation. That land was enormous. There were cattle and horses and acres of corn and cotton. On a good day I could pick seventy pounds of cotton. (My brother Sam got up to two hundred pounds.) I learned to rope the cow and ride the horse. I had a pony of my own. I ran around the land barefoot and learned to shoot a barrel shotgun. If I went out in the woods with my dog and came home with a bird or rabbit, I'd get a pat on the back from Daddy and a hug from Mama. During dinner that night I might get seconds.

We farmed six days a week. There were no such things as parties on Saturday night. Sunday was the True Vine Baptist Church. Church was happy because the music was happy. I was taught that we didn't use just our voices or tambourines to praise God—we used our whole bodies. Wasn't no shame in jumping and shouting for the Lord. Jesus was so good, such a beautiful feeling of pure love in our lives, that he got all of us, body and soul.

I believe it was Jesus that got us through the tough times. We didn't have no irrigation. We didn't have the technology people got today. Any long spell of bad weather meant disaster. And we had many a bad spell. I remember the look on Daddy's face when a long drought killed the cotton crop. There were no other jobs to get—the land was all we had. There were five growing kids to feed. Seeing that they had to do something to keep us from starving, the landowners might give Daddy a few dollars to buy a sack of flour. Mama could make that flour go a long way.

Mama grew the sweet potato, and when she cooked it in the wood stove it came out so sweet we didn't need no sugar on top. Her biscuits were light and fluffy, and her cornbread put a taste in our mouths that had us smiling for the rest of the day. The greens came from the yard. If we had enough money to buy feed, the chicken grew until it was time to wring its neck. That was the kids' job. With blood squirting and feathers flying, we plucked it clean. Then I'd drive the horse and wagon to fetch wood for Mama's stove. She'd cook it juicy good and brown. You never did hear of the salmonella.

You never did hear of the cancer. The food could be sparse, but it was fresh. Mama got up at 4:30 to cook for the sharecroppers, so when the troops—me, my brothers and sisters, and our dad—came in from the fields for lunch, those good beans and rice kept us going for the rest of the day. No one talked about peptic ulcers or irritable bowel syndrome. If someone got really sick, the landowners would rustle up a doctor from somewhere, but that could take days. Better stay healthy.

We were isolated. No newspapers. In my early years, no radio. When I was five I heard talk about America being attacked at Pearl Harbor, but I didn't really understand. The war was in another world. Our world was farming. Our shack was at least a mile away from our nearest neighbor. I could see their shack from the porch of our cabin when the corn wasn't up. But when the crop came in, looking out from our porch I saw nothing but tall, yellow stalks waving at the sun.

We ate fresh nonbird meat but once a year: pork at Christmas. Fact is that there were only two holidays on the plantation—Christmas and Easter. They didn't tell us about Thanksgiving and turkey. And if the crops were right for picking, no one was about to take off no Fourth of July. Christmas was special, not because we had money for presents but because it was time to slaughter a pig.

Because no one had refrigeration, meat had to be eaten quickly. Salt could preserve it some, but nothing tastes better than fresh pork. That meant everyone had to cooperate. My folks and our neighbors would get together a few weeks before Christmas to work out the pig-killing schedule. Mr. Johnson, for example, would slaughter his pig on December 10, keep a good chunk for his family, and give the rest to us neighbors. Five days later Mr. Smith would do the same. Then it was our turn. I spent so much time feeding our pig that he became a friend. Pigs have personalities. Some of them are real friendly and cute. When I was told to cut his throat, I had to pause. Had to think about it. Was the last thing in the world I wanted to do, but despite my feelings, I grabbed hold of the knife and did it.

First music I heard—first music that touched my heart—wasn't made by man. It was the music of the birds. They was singing in the morning and singing at night. They caught my ear and had me wondering about all the creatures made by God. Some crawled and hissed and poisoned you with their bite; others flew and sang and serenaded you with their sweetness. I could follow the different melodies made by different birds. How did they learn their songs? Why were they pretty? When they sang I'd close my eyes so that everything disappeared except those little chirpy songs that made me realize that the world was filled with beautiful sounds.

My folks only had a third-grade education, but that doesn't mean they didn't appreciate talent. There was a man named Henry Smith who had talent. Daddy called him Coot and made sure he came over every Christmas with his two-string guitar. They'd give him wine and have him play. His was the first guitar I ever saw, the first one I ever touched. I watched him pick the thing with his fingers and produce a sound that gave me goose bumps. He sang a song called "Tomorrow Night." Later I learned a blues singer called Lonnie Johnson recorded it. When I first heard Coot we still didn't have no electricity, which meant no radio or records.

Coot would take a wooden chair, sit himself down, put the guitar on his lap, and make it talk. Just two strings. His voice wasn't big, but it went good with the music. Told a story. Made you stop and listen. Naturally he had no drummer, but when he kept time by stomping his foot on the wooden floor, you felt like dancing. You felt like playing and singing yourself.

You best believe I studied Coot. I saw how him and that guitar were connected. It was his woman, his baby, his friend. He stroked it like you stroke a dog. He made it cry and he made it laugh. He had it telling stories that I never heard before. He made me wanna get one.

When Mama bought her first set of screens for our windows, I saw my chance. The screens were a blessing. They protected us from those Louisiana skeeters that were big enough to carry us out the room. Studying them closely, though, seemed like the screens were made from guitar strings. At least that's how I saw it. When my folks were gone I'd take down a screen and pull out a couple of wires from the top. Then I'd string 'em between two tin cans and pretend it was a guitar. I saw how different degrees of tightness gave different sounds. But come morning, Mama and Daddy saw how we was eaten up by the skeeters.

"Who been fooling with the screens?" asked Daddy.

I kept quiet as his eyes darted from child to child before settling on me.

"Why don't you fix these, Buddy, and make sure it don't happen again."

I fixed the screen, but the next day I was fixing up a new contraption—rubber bands stretched out and tacked to the wall. I kept plucking them just like I'd plucked the strings, looking to make the kind of melody that I heard from Coot. Late at night, under the light of a full moon, you'd find me out back sawing off chunks of wood, hoping to put together something that resembled a guitar. Every time, though, I made a mess of it.

But those ringing sounds that Coot made, together with the sweet songs of the birds, never left my head. My head was filled up with music I couldn't play.

After doing our farm work, we walked many miles over gravel roads to school at the True Vine. On the way, a yellow school bus crowded with white kids passed us by. They was on their way to a regular schoolhouse. Sometimes those kids leaned out the window and threw rocks at us. All we could do was jump out the way. I wanted to throw rocks back at them: if a snake bites you, your natural reaction is to crush it dead. But in this case we were outnumbered twenty to one, and there wasn't a chance in hell to retaliate. I didn't think that much about it. I was taught that some white folks were decent and some were downright nasty—just like colored folks. I was taught to avoid the nasty folks of both races.

In our part of Louisiana I never heard stories about the Ku Klux Klan. My father instructed me to address white men as "mister," but he gave me the same instructions about black men. No color deserved more respect than any other.

The most respect I earned came from taming horses. As a youngster, I got me a reputation as someone who could tame a wild animal. Neighbors would bring me their spirited horses. Can't exactly explain how I did it, but it came natural. I could talk to a horse. I could even reason with a horse. I'd say, "I feel that you're wild. I like that you're wild. But listen here, boy. I'm gonna let you take me on one last ride, and then I'm gonna make you behave." I felt a kinship with wild horses—something I understood a little better when I got older and started playing guitar. At a young age, I could see wildness in horses, but I couldn't see it in myself—at least not yet.

I loved baseball, but in the backwoods of Louisiana we didn't have no Little League. We didn't even have a regular hardball. We mashed up cans to hit with a broomstick. We put down rocks for bases. And when it came to listening to games, we went with our dads where we stood in the backyard of the white man who put his radio on his windowsill so we could hear the broadcast. From faraway Brooklyn, we heard how the Dodgers had signed Jackie Robinson, the first black to play in the majors. I could feel the pride in my daddy's heart. I could feel my own heart beating fast when Jackie slapped a double against Warren Spahn of the Boston Braves or stole home against the Phils. When Jackie won Rookie of the Year in 1947, I was only eleven, but you'd think that it was me, along with every black boy in America, who had won the award. I guess the award was for all of us who didn't have the money to buy a mitt or the means to ever see a big league game.

I was too young to remember when Joe Louis fought Max Schmeling in the 1930s, but as a youngster, I was out in the backyard, standing next to my father and grandfather as Louis beat down Billy Conn in the thirteenth round. I remember all of us hooting and hollering for a man who, before Jackie Robinson, was the only American hero with skin the color of ours.

When I think of tough characters, my Daddy's mama comes to mind. I never saw her without a corn pipe in her mouth. When the pipe was smoked out, she'd take the burnt ashes and spread them over her lips. If any of us misbehaved, she was the first to notice. She wouldn't think twice about grabbing the biggest switch off the tree and tanning our bottoms.

On the other hand, Grandpa was more a talker. He liked to tell stories. His favorite—the one that spooked us out—was about the Jesse James days, when white folks was scared to keep their money in the banks. Instead they buried their cash in the ground around certain graves. To keep the black man from digging up that cash, the white man spread a scary story—that ghosts guarded the burial grounds. They said that if you wanted to hunt for the money, you had to leave out shots of whiskey. Give the ghosts whiskey and the ghosts wouldn't bother you none. As a child, these stories messed with me. They crept inside my mind and stayed there. I had dreams of drunken ghosts chasing me all over the chicken house.

Just as bad weather led to the death of the crops, bad circumstances led to the death of people I knew. In the country, death comes often. I remember putting my uncle George in a plain pine box when he died a young man. When I heard that a neighbor, sick of mind, slit his own throat and bled to death, I thought of Christmastime when I had to slit the throat of the pig. Why would anyone slit his own throat?

A little friend of mine, Grant Clark, went hunting in the woods with his dad. Many times I'd done the same thing. But my friend never came back. In a terrible accident that was no one's fault, a gunshot blew off the top of his head. That also haunted my dreams for months afterward.

Life in the country is set by the seasons. In the early months we sit behind the mule as he pulls the tractor to cut furrows in the soil where we'd soon be planting seeds. The mule ain't easy. The mule don't like to be told nothing. "Stubborn as a mule" ain't no lie. The mule likes to fart in your face and piss in the wind. He got the foulest-smelling shit of any animal on earth. And all the time that I'm shouting for him to get done with this dirty work, I'm whipping his fat butt so I can get home and play baseball or run into the woods with my rifle with the hope of bagging a bird for dinner.

Life was steady. We grew the greens, we picked the cotton, we planted the corn. It was a cycle that didn't stop. We watched the sky, hoping that the weather be kind. We watched the fields, hoping the crops would grow.

In a world without changes, one change did come. It didn't keep us from farming like we'd always farmed, but it did give us something we'd never had before.

Light

It was near the end of the 1940s when we finally got an electric line. I was twelve. There was one little light bulb that hung down from the ceiling. Didn't take much of a storm to knock out the power, though. Fact is, that the roof of our shack was so flimsy that any heavy rain created big leaks. Mama had tubs lined up all over to catch the pouring water. Wasn't till much later that I learned what it was like to trust the roof over my head.

The introduction of that little light bulb in our cabin didn't improve life much. But our first piece of electrical equipment, a beat-up used phonograph that played 78 records, changed everything. I thank God that my daddy loved the blues and wanted to hear music when he came out from the fields. I thank God that my daddy had this one record by John Lee Hooker called "Boogie Chillen." That's the record that did it.

In 1949, about when I turned thirteen, "Boogie Chillen" was the biggest hit in the country among black folk—it was by far the biggest hit in the Guy household. Wasn't anything more than one guy playing his electric guitar by himself. Notes were simple. Words were simple. Words didn't even rhyme. But the groove got to me. The mood was so strong that after the song had done played, you had to play it over. When the man said, "Mama told Papa, let the boy boogie woogie," I figured that this John Lee Hooker had to be talking about me. I figured that one way or the other I had to get me a guitar and learn "Boogie Chillen." I knew that inside that song was a mystery I had to know. Once I figured out how the notes worked together, once I memorized all the words and sang the song myself, I'd have a key that would open a door. Didn't know what was on the other side of that door—but I had to find out.

I'd wait for Christmas—not because there were presents, but because Coot was coming. Like everyone who had a guitar, Coot had figured out "Boogie Chillen" and didn't mind when I asked him to play it six or seven times in a row. I'd watch him real careful. Didn't miss nothing. And when he went to drink the wine my daddy had set aside for him, I picked up the guitar and tried to play it myself. My mind heard it, but my fingers couldn't coordinate it. I fumbled. I was frustrated, and when Coot came back, a little happier for the wine, I asked to play the thing again.

"Ain't you ever getting tired of that tune, boy?" he asked.

"No, sir."

Must have been two or three months into the new year when I walked to the little general store. I was on an errand for Mama, buying sugar and salt. I happened to glance outside as an old car pulled up. A skinny man got out. He was wearing a big straw hat, and when I saw what he was carrying under his arm, my heart got to beating so hard I thought it'd bust out my chest.

He was carrying a guitar along with a big black box.

"Who's that?" I asked Artigo, the white man who ran the store.

"Lightnin' Slim."

"He play guitar?"

"Famous for it."

"He gonna play here today?" I asked.

"He will if I give him a bottle of beer."

"Give him two bottles."

He walked in real slow, giving Artigo a big smile.

"That beer cold?" he asked.

Artigo said, "Got a kid here who loves him some guitar."

"What's in that black box?" I asked Lightnin'.

"Just a bunch of wires and tubes. Ain't you never seen no amp?"

"No, sir. What it do?"

"Pushes electricity through the guitar. Makes it louder and stronger. Makes it scream until you can hear it over folk talking. You can hear it over anything. When this here electrical guitar starts to buzzing, folks gonna be flying in here like bees to honey."

"You know 'Boogie Chillen?'" I asked.

"Who don't?"

"You gonna play it?"

"Sure will. You gonna sing along with me, boy?"

"I can't sing."

"Boy, everybody can sing, just like everybody can talk."

As Lightnin' set up I studied the whole situation. Saw him plug the amp thing in the wall. A tiny little light turned red. As he started fingering the guitar, I stood there right in front of him. With the first twang of his guitar a shock ran through my body. The blood inside my head, the blood pumping my heart, the blood running through my limbs—all that blood started into boiling. When Lightnin' began singing, the raw sound of his voice and the jolt of his guitar set me back on my heels. My mouth dropped open so wide a family of flies could have flown in. At that moment I wasn't noticing nothing but Lightnin' Slim playing "Boogie Chillen" on his electrical guitar. He didn't sound like John Lee

Hooker—no one does—but he sounded good. While he played four or five other songs, I didn't move a muscle. I focused my eyes on his fingers like a hound dog focused on a rabbit hole. He played for a half-hour and drank three beers. When he was through and I looked around me, I saw that little store was filled up with people. Don't know where they all came from, but they was there.

Slim winked at me and said, "Out here in country, when I play this here electrical guitar, you can hear it three, four miles in the distance. Didn't I tell you, boy? Folk come buzzin' in like bees to honey."

And then, like the Lone Ranger, he packed his guitar and amp, walked out to his car, and rode off into the sunset.

I knew about the Lone Ranger because every few weeks Artigo would let us black boys pile into the back of his pickup and he would drive us to a movie theater in a little town ten miles away. Fact is, me and Artigo's son had been good friends as little boys. When we got older, though, we was told that whites and blacks couldn't be buddies. He didn't like that, and neither did I, but that's how it was.

At the movies blacks had to sit upstairs while the whites went downstairs closer to the big screen. I loved seeing Gene Autry and Roy Rogers riding their horses and gunning down cattle rustlers. When Gene picked up his guitar and sang around the campfire, my eyes went right to his fingers. How did he make that nice, calming sound? Lightnin' Slim and John Lee Hooker didn't calm me down. They worked me up. I liked being worked up, but I also liked a guitar that was smooth and easy. Those cowboy songs were like lullabies. You had to love a lullaby. Because I wasn't a bad lasso man myself, I got a big kick out of Lash LaRue and the other cow-boys who knew how to work a rope. I liked all them lasso artists and gunslingers.

Back in our little country shack I kept close to the phonograph. After John Lee Hooker, we got some records by Lightnin' Hopkins. There was "Lightnin's Boogie" and "Moanin' Blues." Lightnin' was a little softer than John Lee. He had a different kind of twang. When he played, his little notes seemed to be walking, like when I would walk down by the bayou. When he sang, he was telling me a story, almost like my daddy or uncle telling a story. I believed every word he said. And when those words was put to a rhythm and the rhythm got my foot to tapping and my heart to singing, all I could do was take that needle and put it back at the beginning of the record so I could hear the man do it again.

The general store where I saw Lightnin' Slim had a jukebox that held all the records I liked so well. That's where I first heard Muddy Waters singing "Rollin' Stone." Like John Lee and Lightnin', he cracked open my soul to everything he said in his songs. I felt like I knew him.

"Where does Muddy Waters live?" I asked Artigo.

"Chicago. All these guys live up there in Chicago."

"Chicago far away?"

"Real far."

Artigo said the harmonica man called Little Walter lived in Chicago too. He pressed a button, and I watched as one of Walter's records came on.

"Sounds like a woman crying, don't it?" said Artigo.

"Yes, sir," I said.

"Or a man begging," he added.

I wasn't sure what he meant.

"You ain't ever begged for it, boy, have you?"

"I guess not," I said.

"You will."

I did.

It happened around the same time all this music started kicking in.

Now when girls fall in love for the first time, they'll tell you that the music they happened to be hearing at that time is the prettiest in the world. When boys start into moving with the sex urge, music also goes along with that feeling. Girl or boy, that's the music that's gonna travel with you for the rest of your life. It gonna talk to you, walk with you, slip into bed with you, and wake you up in the morning. The seeds of that music are planted in fertile soil.

For me that music was the blues. Everyone knows that the blues can be both sad and happy. But the blues is also sexy. When the blues gets inside you, it stirs up your nature to get down and dirty.

In the country, especially in Louisiana where the ground is moist and muddy, we had to get down standing up. We had to learn to make love from a vertical position. That ain't easy, but baby, where there's a will, there's a way. First time it happened I was probably fifteen. It could be awkward, but it also could be good, especially if you find a little bench where your honey could raise up her leg.

When it came to music, I was wild. When I'd learn Lightnin' Slim was coming back through or a new Big Boy Crudup tune was loaded on Artigo's jukebox, I'd run like the wind. When it to came to girls, though, I wasn't wild. I was careful. That's 'cause my grandma was careful to warn me that women are like plants in the jungle: many are beautiful and contain ingredients that can heal your body, but others, just as beautiful, contain poison.

"The wrong woman," said Grandma, "can kill you. Or treat you in a way that will make you wanna kill yourself."

As a young buck, I was following my nature—and my nature was strong—but I was also following Grandma's advice. I was avoiding the crazy girls, the ones who'd tell everyone their business—and yours. I liked the quiet ones who seemed happy just to enjoy the boy-girl feeling that makes life worthwhile.

While I was still on the farm, though, it wasn't sex that was most on my mind but baseball and music. And if it came down to choosing between the two, music was the winner. If me and the boys was hitting the tin can with Mama's mop stick, for example, and we heard a radio playing Smokey Hogg's "Good Morning Little Schoolgirl," I'd shout out, "Rain delay!" and run to the radio. The rain delay lasted as long as the announcer kept playing blues. If the weather was clear, the radio could pick up a station from far-off Tennessee, where they might be playing Willie Mabon's "I Don't Know," J. B. Lenoir's "Korea Blues," or Howlin' Wolf's "Moanin' at Midnight."

In the catalogues we got from Montgomery Ward and Sears Roebuck I studied the pages with musical instruments. I studied pictures of guitars like other boys studied pictures of half-naked ladies. I had to have me one. There wasn't a chance in the world to get twenty dollars to send off for a new guitar, but one Christmas something happened that was nearly as good.

As usual, we had our dinner of fresh pork along with fresh greens, beans, and sweet potatoes. In the evening Coot showed up with his guitar. After drinking more than his fair share of wine, he broke into a sped-up version of Joe Liggins's "Honeydripper." That got everyone up to dancing. The weather had been right that winter, and it looked like the land would yield Daddy a decent penny.

"Henry," said Daddy, calling Coot by his right name, "I been knowing your daddy Jim Smith for many a year. How old was you when he got you this here guitar?"

"I'd say twelve."

"Just about the age of my boy Buddy."

"Yes, sir."

"And I'm guessing that this ain't the only guitar you have."

"You guessing right. Got me another at home. That's my dry stick for a rainy day."

"Well, looks like a little rain today, Coot, 'cause I'm prepared to buy this here guitar from you."

When Daddy said those words, my heart started thumping hard against my chest.

"I couldn't let you have it for less than five dollars, Mr. Guy."

"Well, I got me four dollars just waiting to warm the inside of your pocket."

"Four dollars and a little change might do it."

"I can find some change," said Daddy, searching through his pockets. "I can find a quarter."

"That quarter," said Coot, "gonna be lonely by itself. It needs another quarter go with it."

"I got a dime to go with it. I got four dollars and thirty-five cent. You can take that money and buy you enough wine to last till the weather turns warm."

Daddy handed over the money, and Coot handed me the guitar.

Life ain't never been the same since.

"Before you go, Coot," I said, "please show me how to play 'Boogie Chillen.'"

"Simple," said Coot. "You just lock in these here notes."

He showed me the notes. At first my mind couldn't talk to my fingers. I had to ask Coot to show me again. By then, though, he was deep into his wine and didn't wanna bother.

"Please," I begged. "I gotta learn 'Boogie Chillen.'"

"This is the last time, boy."

He showed me how to move my left hand up and down the neck of the guitar and which of the two strings to pluck with my right hand.

I had it. I played it. My sisters and brothers were happy to hear me play, but after the fourth or fifth time they said it was okay to stop. I didn't stop, though, because Coot was good and drunk and in no condition to show me a third time how to finger the song. So like a fool in love with a lady he couldn't leave alone, I couldn't leave the song alone. I wouldn't stop playing it. I played it for an hour, and then for two. I played it walking around the back of the house, walking out through the cornfields, walking down by the bayou and then up into the woods. I kept playing it because I was scared silly that if I stopped, I'd forget it. I had to play this song until it was as much a part of me as my liver or my beating heart. When the hour turned late and I couldn't hold my eyes open any longer, I went to sleep with the guitar in my arms, afraid that when morning came, the song would be gone and I'd never be able to play the song again. So I hummed it in my head and prayed that I'd keep playing it in my dreams. When I woke up, I grabbed my guitar, wondering whether the notes of "Boogie Chillen" would still be there.

They were.

Mitchell

At the start of the 1950s I was sitting on a porch in Baton Rouge, playing that same guitar my daddy bought from Coot. I was fifteen years old and had moved from Lettsworth to live with my big sister Annie Mae. I was about to enroll in high school. Mama and Daddy encouraged this move for one simple reason: they wanted me to go further than they did. There was no high school in Lettsworth, and if I was to advance my education, Baton Rouge was the only place. I was a little uneasy about the move because our shack on that great big plantation was all I ever knew. Back then Baton Rouge couldn't have had many more than 120,000 people. Compared to where I was coming from, though, that was a lot. It wasn't no New York or Chicago or even New Orleans or Memphis, but it would take some getting used to. Looking at it now, I see it as a kicked-back rural kind of city, a country town, but when I arrived fresh off the farm, there was an adjustment to make. And that lil' ol' two-string guitar helped me make the adjustment.

Out there on the porch I was fooling with a new song by John Lee Hooker called "I'm in the Mood." Every John Lee song said something to me.

"You sound like you're serious about the guitar," said a man passing by. His skin was black as coal.

"I am, sir."

"That there guitar looks mighty beat up," he said.

"I got it from a guy who had it for a long time."

"I see it's only got two strings. Ain't guitars supposed to have six?"

"I think so," I said, "but I'm happy to have any guitar at all."

"I bet if you had a good guitar, you'd get more better playing it. You'd probably get more better in a hurry."

"Maybe so."

"Say, son, you gonna be around tomorrow?"

"Yes, sir."

"Tomorrow's Saturday and I don't gotta work. I'll pass by here tomorrow and look for you."

"I'll be here."

Had no idea what the man had in mind, but I was back on the porch on Saturday, still fooling with "I'm in the Mood."

In early afternoon that same man passed by.

"You ready?" he asked.

"Ready for what, sir?"

"Ready to get you a guitar."

"How am I gonna do that? I got no money for a guitar."

"I do. Let's go downtown to where they sell them things."

And just like that, the man took me downtown in his raggedy old car, walked me into a music store, and had me pick out a Harmony six-string guitar.

"How much is that?" he asked the store owner.

"Fifty-two dollars."

To me, $52 was all the money in the world. Who in hell had $52 to spend on a guitar?

This man did. He reached in his pocket, pulled the cash out of his wallet, and handed it to the owner. The owner carefully counted the money. It was right. Then he handed me the guitar.

All I could say was "thank you." I thanked the man who bought it, I thanked the owner of the store, and in my silent mind I thanked the Good Lord in heaven.

On the way back to Annie Mae's house, the man stopped to buy himself a quart of beer. At Annie Mae's he and I sat on the porch while I played and he drank. The Harmony was made of golden brown wood with a tone so pretty you could cry. It was clear and pure and strong. I didn't exactly know what to do with them strings, but I was learning fast. The strings were tight and felt good to the tips of my fingers. Wasn't long before I was playing "Boogie Chillen" with all six strings. What a difference between two and six! Was like I had a whole orchestra in my hands.

Before long Annie Mae arrived, talkin' 'bout, "What's this here country boy doing with a shiny new guitar?"

The man said it was a gift and offered Annie Mae some beer.

"Don't look like you got enough for two," she said. "I better run and get us another quart."

"I'm doing the buying today," said the man, who got up, went off to the liquor store, and returned with more beer.

As they was drinking and I was playing, Annie Mae got an idea.

"You know where Lettsworth is?" she asked the man.

"Sure enough," he said. "Know it well."

"Well, it's Saturday night. Let's ride on out there in that car of yours and visit our folks. We can bring 'em some beer and they can hear this little brother of mine playing on his new guitar. What you say?"

The man said yes. I said yes. We put a dollar's worth of gas in his car and rode the fifty miles north from Baton Rouge to

Lettsworth. We pulled right up in front of the wooden cabin where I'd been raised.

My dog started barking his friendly bark. Out in the country no one had locks on their doors. Your dog was the only warning you needed to hear whether it was a stranger or friend come to call. My dog was licking my face when Daddy came out to greet us.

"My, my, my," he said. "Annie Mae and Buddy. This is a right beautiful surprise." Then he looked at the man and said, "Ain't you Mitchell? Mitchell Young?"

"That's me," said the man. "And ain't you Sam?"

"I'm Sam Guy and you're the same Mitchell I grew up with when we was little boys."

The two men shook hands before giving each other a good hug.

"Mitchell just bought Buddy a new guitar," said Annie Mae.

"Knowing he was my son?" asked my daddy.

"Knowing nothing about that," said Mitchell. "I heard something in this boy that said he needed a real guitar."

By then Mama had come out of the house and taken me in her arms. She'd heard the whole story.

"Lord, have mercy," she said. "Ain't this a beautiful night!"

The Rouge

The idea was simple: move to Baton Rouge, go to high school, and learn something better than farming.

"Farming ain't getting you nowhere," said Daddy. "You gotta get some schooling, boy. We gonna be living hand to mouth long as we on this land. The business is set up to keep us down. But I don't want you down, son. I want you up."

Sister Annie Mae was happy to take me in. She had a decent job at LSU, and her husband worked at Standard Oil. She gave me fifteen cent a day for my little expenses and a rollaway bed where I slept in the front room. Annie Mae was wonderful to me. She was also something of a mess, but what I'd call a beautiful mess. Come Saturday night, she'd be deep into the wine and beer. She could get wild. Many were the times when the police had to put her in jail for getting crazy in the barrooms. She never did get violent on me, though, and for those first months that I was away from home she became my second mom.

I finished out eighth grade at McKinley High and had every intention of going on with my schooling. Then one day Annie Mae came running in the house. She had just been out to Lettsworth. Her eyes were wet with tears.

"What's wrong?" I asked.

"Mama just took a stroke."

"What's a stroke?" I had to ask.

"They say it's when the blood doesn't flow to your brain right. Everything gets thrown off."

"I don't understand."

"She can hardly talk. Can hardly move."

"Is Mama about to die?" I asked.

"I don't think so, but I don't really know. All I know is that the doctor says she'll never be the same."

That same day I went out to Lettsworth and saw that Mama couldn't talk and could hardly walk. Her mouth was droopy and her eyes were far away. She'd always been a woman up and working before anyone. She looked after her husband and kids with all the love and care in the world, and seeing her like this broke my heart. Broke Daddy's heart too. Never seen my father look helpless before—he always knew what to do.

"Doctor says ain't nothing to do," said Daddy.

But I knew what I had to do.

I had to go home.

When Mama took her stroke, everything changed. She could no longer smile. I'd seen that smile my whole life. It was my sunshine. That smile told me the world was alright and that I could get through anything. I'd be hungry for that smile for the rest of my life.

We tried, but without Mama we couldn't go back to our old lives. I left Baton Rouge and went home to work the fields, but the Guy family could never be what it once was.

One night after we'd been picking cotton all day, me, Daddy, and my brothers were sitting around, tired in our bodies and our minds. Mom was in the bed. Daddy went and took her hand.

"You know, Isabell," he said, "you'd never let any of us come home to a dirty shirt or a dirty sheet or a dirty dish. Never did happen. You never did miss a day of work. And on most days you did more work than three or four strong men. Ain't that right, honey?"

Mama couldn't answer, but Daddy kept talking.

"You gonna be all right," he said. "We all here for you. We waiting on you, Isabell. We waiting for as long as it takes. We right here. I know you hear what I'm saying."

Daddy looked at Mama in her eyes. I thought I saw her eyes smiling, but her mouth couldn't make a smile.

We went on wishing and praying that Mama would return to her old self. Even though the doctor said that wasn't gonna happen, we wanted to believe it would. We had to believe it would. We had to hold on to hope.

But hope lasts only so long before cold reality sets in. Reality told us that living on a plantation with a very sick woman wasn't fair to that woman. She needed to see a doctor on a regular basis.

Daddy decided to leave the plantation and move the family to Baton Rouge. Him and us kids getting different jobs would mean more money to help care for Mama. The landowners were sorry to see us go—we were their best workers. They wished us good luck and loaned us a truck to move our stuff. Daddy found a small house to rent, I went back to sleep on a rollaway at Annie Mae's, and our life in Lettsworth was over.

My life in Baton Rouge began and ended with me working. I worked a conveyor belt in a beer factory, where the temperature had to be 110. The job was monotonous and taxed me a hundred more times than working on the farm. On the farm I was outside. I could hear the birds and see the animals. I dealt with live crops growing or dying according to the weather. I had the sky over my head, not a dirty ceiling in a factory that smelled like it hadn't been cleaned in a year. Farm work was hard, but I was seeing that farm work could feel free. This factory work felt like jail. The job didn't last long.

Service station work was a little better. At least I was outside. I've always been good with cars, so dealing with them was okay, except during the dog days of summer. In those years customers couldn't pump their own gas. The attendants did the pumping. That was easy and so was checking the tires. But when it came to checking the battery and water, the second I popped open the hood of the car the 96-degree day turned to 120. I did good not to pass out from the fumes. The average sale in those days, when gas cost twenty cents a gallon, was under a buck. The owner of the station also had me doing tow truck service. Before long I knew every street and back alley in Baton Rouge.

I also found work at LSU. I was a maintenance man. The atmosphere on a college campus was calm, and I didn't mind cleaning and sweeping and driving their utility vehicles to do all kinds of odd jobs. They even had a tractor I could handle good as anyone.

For the next years the routine would have me working at the school during the day and at the gas station at night. In between this work, though, my passion for the guitar heated up even more. The records from jukeboxes kept me locked into Muddy and Lightnin', Wolf and Little Walter. Jimmy Reed was coming up strong. They said he could blow harp and pick his guitar at the same time. His main guitarist, though, Eddie Taylor, gave off a twangy sound different from anyone. Reed had a nasal voice, thick like Mississippi mud, that sang over the funky rhythm to where you had to reach for a drink or a woman.

I loved these people. But I loved them from far off. I dreamed of seeing them, but they didn't come to Baton Rouge. In the meantime, though, a famous guitarist did come, and I did go see him. I had heard his record, and I liked him. I knew he was good. Until I saw him up close and in person, though, I didn't know that he would change all my ideas of what it meant to play the blues. I didn't know that he'd rearrange my brain and set me soaring in a new direction.

Where Is He? Where the Hell Is He?

On the little radio that Annie Mae kept in the kitchen, I was listening to Dizzy Dean on Mutual Radio broadcasting a Saturday game between the Brooklyn Dodgers and the Braves. The night before, I was up late listening to the St. Louis Cardinals–New York Giants game. I closed my eyes and imagined what it was like to see Stan Musial or Willie Mays smash a baseball clean out of the park.

After the game was over, me, Annie Mae, and a friend with a car drove over to the School of Agriculture at LSU, where they had a department that taught you to be a butcher. The teacher showed the students how to cut up the choice parts of a pig. When class was over, they'd throw the pig's head, chitlins, and feet into a barrel. They considered that stuff garbage. Well, we went through the garbage, gathered up the parts they discarded, loaded 'em into a big box, and sold it off cheap to the folks in the neighborhood who knew how to cook it.

The only other little extra money I got came from music. That didn't begin all too good. Remember, when I left the farm for

Baton Rouge, you couldn't find anyone more country than me. On top of that, I have a naturally shy nature. Never been good at going out and introducing myself to people I don't know. As a kid and a teenager, I stayed quiet most all of the time. Didn't feel like I had nothing to say.

When there was downtime at the service station, I picked up that Harmony guitar and played. Might be Lightnin' Hopkins's "Fast Life Woman" or Muddy's "Hoochie Coochie Man" or Elmore James's "Dust My Broom." These were the kind of songs I was always trying to learn. The station owner would hear me and say, "You oughta get paid for doing that."

"Who's gonna pay me?"

"Well, keep playing and someday someone's gonna hear you and wanna pay you. I *guaran-goddamn-tee* you."

Wasn't no more than a week later when this big mountain of a man drove up to the station just when I was trying to play some Jimmy Reed.

"Ain't bad," he said. "My name's Big Poppa. Who you?"

"Buddy. Buddy Guy."

"Well, look here, Buddy. I got me a band and been looking for another guitarist. You free tonight?"

"Yes, sir."

"We playing up at a barroom called Sitman's. You know 'Work with Me, Annie'?"

"Hank Ballard and the Midnighters," I said. "They used to be called the Royals. Yes, sir, I know it real good. Know all the notes."

"But can you sing it?"

"I know all the words."

"Be at Sitman's at nine o'clock tonight."

I thought I was ready. But when I agreed to play with Big Poppa, I didn't know what playing music in front of strangers would be like. When I walked into Sitman's, the joint was jammed—wall-to-wall people waiting to hear something good.

"Found me a youngblood," said Sitman to the crowd, "who can sing one of your favorites."

The band broke into "Work with Me, Annie." There wasn't no rehearsal, but that didn't bother me. I knew the tune. And I knew just when to jump in and start singing. What bothered me, though, was facing the audience. I just couldn't. Shyness got the best of me. So I turned my back on the crowd and sang to the wall.

"You crazy, boy!" screamed Big Poppa. "You out your goddamn mind! You can't play to no fuckin' wall!"

More he yelled at me, shyer I got until it would have taken a shotgun to my head to make me turn around.

When we got through with the song, Big Poppa said, "You fired!"

"But I just got started!" I protested.

"You got started on the wrong foot—and turned in the wrong direction. Get the fuck out!"

I got out, felt terrible about the whole thing, and went home to bed. Next morning I told a friend, Raymond Brown, about how I'd messed up.

"Well, Buddy, you ain't gonna mess up a second time. This time I'm going with you to Sitman's. I got just the right medicine to loosen you up until you ain't afraid to look the people dead in the eye."

"Would rather look at the wall."

"You keep looking at the wall and you'll wind up hitting your head against it. You too good to look at the wall. You got to look at the folks paying to hear you play."

If it wasn't for Raymond Brown, I would never have gone back to Sitman's. He had enough confidence for the both of us. He also had a bottle of Dr. Tichenor's Antiseptic medicine, usually used to treat cuts and wounds or to rinse out your mouth. He poured the stuff into a glass.

"Drink this down," he said, "and you'll be shouting out the good news in no time."

I drank one glass—and then a second. After the second I felt like I could spread wings and fly to the moon. I could get on that bandstand and, despite the dirty looks from Big Poppa, tell him I was ready to sing "Annie" face first.

"This is your last chance, boy," he said.

"Just hit it," I said.

I hit it hard. Sang that song for all it was worth. Found me a pretty girl and focused all my attention on her. Her smiling lips were a lot more inviting than the back wall. Yes, sir, with help from my friend Raymond Brown, I faced the people—and I've been facing them ever since.

Big Poppa played harp. He was no Little Walter. This was the time when Little Walter's "Juke" had taken over the radio stations and the jukeboxes. All you heard was "Juke." It was just music—no singing—but Walter was singing through that harmonica like no one had ever sung before. He made the thing laugh and cry. Before Little Walter, harmonicas cost a dime. Folks looked at them as toys. After Little Walter, harmonicas cost $5. Folks looked at them as instruments.

Seeing I was good for his band, Big Poppa took me to all the roadhouses in and around Baton Rouge, joints like the Lakeland Lodge, Rockin' Lucky, and Joe Bradley's Dew Drop Inn. If we went outside the city for a little gig, Poppa took his Oldsmobile 98. He was so big that he took up the whole front seat. Poppa's wife was so jealous that she wouldn't let no other woman go with us, not even my sister Annie Mae, who liked to hear me play. But we'd sneak Annie Mae in the backseat and take her anyway. Sometimes Big Poppa would give me $2 a night, sometimes $3. But I didn't care—I was playing.

I was also listening to other Baton Rouge players. Lightnin' Slim, who I'd heard in Lettsworth, was around. Schoolboy Cleve and Rafel Neal were his first harmonica players before Lazy Lester. Lazy liked to say, "I ain't lazy, I'm just tired."

In Baton Rouge they was always talkin' 'bout New Orleans. I knew that Smiley Lewis, Lloyd Price, Fats Domino, and Shirley and Lee were making records down there. Before long Little Richard would be recording in that same city. Richard was the one who sped up the music until they started calling it rock and roll. New Orleans had all kinds of music happening, and you'd think because it was only eighty miles from where I was staying, I'd be down there a lot. But I wasn't. Had no reason to. Nothing was calling me down to New Orleans. Wasn't part of my world. Never even went there. But it was a New Orleans artist who rearranged my thinking.

It wasn't B. B. King, who was a Memphis artist. Don't get me wrong—I was in love with B. B.'s style from the time I heard "Three O'Clock Blues." His guitar had a ring and a sting that snapped back my head. His sound gave me chills.

This other guitar man, though, gave me something I didn't get from B. B. This artist showed me how to present myself to the public. He showed me how to put on a show. More than any guitarist I can name, he taught me how to attract and excite a crowd. His name was Guitar Slim.

Slim had a record out, "The Things I Used to Do," that, after "Boogie Chillen," became the biggest record of my life. I say that because I played the thing night and day for many years. Hell, I'm still playing it. Loved that song like I loved my mama. Ray Charles, who back then was living in New Orleans, arranged and produced it for Slim. Ray also played piano on the track. Ray's production was perfect. Within months of the song's release there wasn't a guitarist in the South that couldn't play "The Things I Used to Do."

Minute I heard that Guitar Slim was performing at the Masonic Temple in Baton Rouge I ran over. I was the first guy in line to buy a ticket. Cost fifty cent. The hall had a big ballroom. I knew the place would be packed with dancers, and I wanted to be right up on the bandstand. I wanted to see the man's hands when he played the guitar. Didn't take long before the crowd arrived. Soon it was full. Folks pushing and shoving, but I wasn't moving. Kept my spot so I could see and hear everything. Eight o'clock came and went. Then nine o'clock. Then nine-thirty. At about a quarter to ten the band came on stage and started playing the opening notes of "The Things I Used to Do." Man, my heart skipped a beat. It was like someone had poured a quart of whiskey down my throat. I was warm all over. I heard the music alright, but I didn't see Guitar Slim. The guitar kept playing, but there was no guitarist. I thought to myself, *Where is he? Where the hell is he?*

As the song kept blasting, the question kept running through my mind. I didn't know what was going on. I'd paid my fifty cent and wanted to see the man behind the music.

Finally, I heard a buzz in the crowd. Everyone turned around. From the back of the ballroom, coming through the door, was this giant fat man carrying a guitarist on his shoulders. The guitarist was Slim, playing like his life was on the line. Mounted atop the huge guy, Slim looked like a baby. But he was no baby. He was slick as grease and dressed to kill—flaming red suit, flaming red shoes, flaming red-dyed hair. He made his way through the room until everyone was in a stoned fury. When he jumped down from the shoulders of his man, I saw that his guitar was a beat-up Strat that looked like it'd been through two world wars. He wore the guitar low on his hip like a gunslinger. His guitar strap was made of fish wire and the cord to his amp had to be three hundred feet long. Before this, my idea of a guitarist was Lightnin' Slim, who sat when he played. Lightnin' was the one who told me that the guitar was designed to be played sitting down. It fit on your lap. That's where I figured a guitar belonged.

Guitar Slim never sat down. He played his guitar between his legs, played it behind his back, played it *on* his back, played it jumping off the stage, played it hanging from the rafters. Wasn't nothing Slim wouldn't do and nowhere he wouldn't go with that beautiful old Strat of his.

The Strat was strong. Its one-piece Maple neck was made with steel and could take a beating. The tough construction allowed Slim to sling it around his hip like a bag of potatoes. I liked how he treated it rough, because that treatment got into the feeling of the music. The music was blistering. It was like the Strat was saying, "Go ahead, throw me around, beat me up, I can take all you got and still sound like a screaming angel from heaven."

Guitar Slim's show thrilled me. He wasn't bending the strings but straight lickin' 'em. I had heard a little of T-Bone Walker, B. B.'s idol and one of the first to plug the guitar into the wall. I liked how T-Bone could chord the instrument. Slim didn't know no chords. He was single pickin' with only two fingers, but those two fingers were causing a riot.

After the show I hung around just to get a better look at the man. As he was walking off stage a guy stopped him and said, "Hey, Slim, how many different colors of shoes you got?"

"Got me all the colors of the rainbow," said Slim. "Got me a dye for every color so I can match my hair to my shoes."

"You crazy, man," said the man.

"Oh yeah?" said Slim. "Well, one day every goddamn motherfucker you see gonna be dressed crazy like me. That's the way the world be changing. Me, I'm just ahead of all you other cats."

I thought about those words a dozen years later when I turned up in San Francisco and saw the flower-power hippie children dressed up all crazy in every color of the rainbow.

"Hey, Slim," said another fan. "You so good, man, I'm giving you a taste of my whiskey. Matter of fact, I'm giving you a whole pint."

"Thank you, good brother." And with that, Slim sucked down the entire pint.

"Better watch it there, Mr. Guitar Slim," said a pretty-legged lady in a tight skirt. "Hear tell you drink too much. Keep drinking like that and you ain't gonna be livin' long."

"Maybe so, darlin', but for every regular day you live, I be livin' three."

I followed Slim outside and watched him get into his big Cadillac and roar off into the night. Never did say a word to him because, frankly speaking, I wouldn't know what to say except "thank you."

Guitar Slim showed me to how to play the guitar in front of people. Whatever he did, I wanted to do. The excitement he caused, I wanted to cause. The pleasure he gave, I wanted to give. I wanted a Strat that I could beat up. I wanted a big crowd that I could drive wild.

I wanted to be Guitar Slim.

Love in the Mud

Blues can bring you up or put you down, but in almost every blues, somewhere in the song there's a female in the room, a female about to do you wrong, do you right, storm out of your life, or let you love her down.

Blues, love, and lovemaking are all carved from the same piece of wood. They come from the same place. I felt that place during my teen years in Baton Rouge. The blues had stormed my soul while my body was craving what all bodies crave when the nature starts boiling your blood. The nature has you hunting the way men been hunting ever since Adam got a load of Eve.

Back on the plantation there were more girls than boys. The girls were working right beside us and didn't have the time, means, or money to get all prettied up. I noticed them, of course, and like I said before, I had one, but that didn't make me very experienced. In the country, boys didn't learn how to love so good.

I remember a friend telling me about taking his girl out to a muddy field on a dark night. Moon was all covered with clouds, a fog was coming in thick, and he couldn't see in front of him.

She's down there on the ground when he goes to get between her legs, but instead of putting it in her pussy, he puts it in the mud.

"Oh, baby," he says. "You so good. Feels so good."

"You don't even have it in me," she say.

"I don't?"

"No, fool, you don't."

"Oh."

So he takes it out of the mud, cleans it off, and puts it where it belongs. She starts to a-moaning but he ain't saying nothin'.

"What's the matter, honey?" she asks. "Ain't it good to you?"

"To tell you the truth, the mud feels better."

I worried that the girls I saw during my few months at McKinley High would think I was too country. They were pretty and wore clothes that showed off what they had. And they had plenty. I spent my day looking but didn't say a word.

That changed a little when I got into playing the guitar. Ladies like musicians. Some of them came up to me with a smile or a wink. Naturally, I got excited. But my shyness didn't go away all that fast, and neither did my feeling that I better be cautious. All around me I saw women getting pregnant—women my age. The men didn't think nothing of it. Sometimes they married the woman and sometimes they just walked away.

"You ain't ever gonna walk away if you get a woman pregnant," my daddy said. "You gonna take care of her and the child."

That's when I started taking a harder look at older women. Thinking it through, I decided they was a safer bet. As lovers, I saw they could be better than the younger ones. They didn't mind teaching me what to do and how to do it. I liked learning. I liked how they showed me to take my time. I especially liked the ones who had already been married 'cause they wasn't looking to have a baby. Matter of fact, having been through it, they were looking *not* to have a baby.

One of those ladies, a wonderful woman named Phyllis, had two little girls and asked me to babysit them. I was happy to say yes and even happier to say yes again when Phyllis invited me into her bed. My idea, though, that ladies with kids wouldn't be wanting any more didn't prove entirely true. When I was seventeen, Phyllis had a little girl by me—Judy—and three years later we had another girl she called Dorqus. I was pleased with these babies and also pleased that Phyllis wasn't interested in getting married. She was the kind of woman who liked being independent. She didn't put no strings on me, she said she would care for these babies by herself, and I was grateful not to be tied down.

Sometime during my days in Baton Rouge I was at my sister's playing my guitar—by then I'd gotten a Les Paul Gibson—when who should turn up but Lawrence Chalk, a man we called Shorty. He came from Baton Rouge but later moved to Baton Rouge before going off to Chicago, leaving his wife behind.

"Shorty," I said, "good to see you, man. What you doin' back in town?"

"My wife, Buddy. She got killed. Terrible accident."

"That's awful, Shorty. I'm really sorry. Out of respect, I'll put away this here guitar."

"Don't do that, Buddy. You keep playing. I see Annie Mae has opened a nice bottle of wine. I got no reason not to get drunk. And the more I drink, the more I got to hear me some music."

I played "The Things I Used to Do."

"Well, that'll get me to drinking," said Shorty. "That'll do."

As Shorty went to drinking, I kept playing. Soon he and Annie Mae were dancing up a storm. It was like that for another couple of hours.

"Hey, Buddy," he said, "how 'bout Jimmy Reed? You know his songs?"

"I'm learning them."

"He lives in Chicago. All of 'em do. Muddy Waters. Little Walter. Howlin' Wolf. They all up there where I live."

"So I've heard."

"Why don't you come up there?"

"What am I gonna do up there?"

"Find a street corner and play your guitar. Someone's sure to hear you."

"I don't got no money."

"Save some," said Shorty. "Save enough for the train ride. And when you get there, you can sleep where I can stay."

"You mean that?"

"Wouldn't say it if I didn't mean it."

"How would I find a job up there?"

"More jobs there than here, Buddy. Where you working now?"

"LSU."

"All kinds of colleges in Chicago. What you getting now?"

"Twenty-nine dollars a week."

"You'll get twice that in Chicago."

"Twice?"

"Maybe three times. That's why everyone's going to Chicago. Chicago's the place, man."

Shorty's words hung heavy. Couldn't get them off my mind. Chicago was far enough away to be on the moon. Had no family in Chicago. Besides, no one in our family had ever gone off like that. None of us had been out of Louisiana. But knowing that Shorty was living in Chicago planted a seed in my heart. Took a while, but the seed started to grow.

Started thinking that if I ever did go to Chicago, I'd have to play better. So I went to see about taking music lessons.

The music lesson man wanted to give me a book that was hard to understand. Looked like math to me. Didn't look like no fun.

"This is the book," he said, "that you need to begin with."

"Well, sir," I said, "I've already begun."

"You began with another book?" he asked.

"Begun with a *different* kind of book."

"What's it called?"

"'Hoochie Coochie Man' by Muddy Waters."

"That ain't no book. That's a song."

"Yeah, but I can read it like a book. It's been teaching me like a book. I know every last thing in it."

"But you need *this* book," the man said.

After looking it over I said, "Not sure I do. Think I'll stick with Muddy."

Without the music book I was doing okay in the little joints around Baton Rouge. I wasn't making no money, but I had a little reputation. And after seeing Guitar Slim I got me a long cord and started out playing in the alley and then strutting in from the street to the club like the man himself. I had to carry a smoldering iron with me 'cause if my wire broke, I didn't have the money to buy another one—just smoldered the wire together.

Whether I was up playing in the roadhouses, working at the gas station, doing odd jobs at LSU, or in the bed loving on Phyllis, my thoughts kept going back to Chicago. I didn't think I was good enough to make a living picking the guitar up there, but I sure did dream of getting a glimpse of Muddy and Walter and them driving around in their fine cars. I just wanted to sneak a peek at the big mansions where they lived. And naturally, I dreamed of going to some beautiful nightclub and hearing them play in the flesh.

But those were dreams. Dreams weren't real. At the same time, though, I could get crazy with dreams. The dreams went on for some time until I got the nerve to mention it to my daddy.

"Daddy," I said, "you think I'm crazy to be thinking of going up there to Chicago to stay with Lawrence Chalk?"

"Shorty? Shorty living in Chicago?"

"Yes, sir. He likes it real fine."

"He thinks you could find some work?"

"That what he says."

"You think you could make money with your guitar in Chicago?"

"No, I wouldn't even try. I'd find me a regular job. Shorty says there's jobs to be had there."

"Well, if you do play your guitar, play 'Stagger Lee.' You know 'Stagger Lee,' son?"

"I heard it."

"If you going to Chicago, you best learn it."

"I'll do my best."

"I know you will."

They had a radio station in Baton Rouge called WXOK where Ray Meadows worked. His deejay name was Diggy Doo, and he liked me. Because they had microphones and a little studio, he told me I could make a sample of my music. Later I'd learn that's called a "demo." I'd written a song called "Baby Don't You Wanna Come Home." It wasn't going to compete with J. B. Lenoir or John Lee Hooker, but it didn't sound too bad when I heard the playback.

"What are you going to do with this, Buddy?" asked Diggy.

"Probably nothing," I said, "but I've been half-thinking of going to Chicago. Just trying to get my nerve up."

"Well, if you do go, look up Leonard Chess."

"Who's he?"

"Man who runs Chess Records."

"Where Muddy and them make their records?"

"The same."

"How you know him?"

"He comes through here once a year or so. He makes it a point to tell me what new Chess Records are coming out. I do him the favor of playing 'em."

"So y'all are friends?"

"Wouldn't say friends," said Diggy, "but business associates. I know him well enough to write a letter for you to give him. If you decide to go to Chicago, I'll give you his address. You can play him this demo."

"Think he'd like it?"

"Hard to tell what other people are going to like, Buddy, but I like it. I like it a lot."

Encouragement was coming at me, and I needed it real bad. Even as I turned twenty-one, I still wasn't what you'd call a real man of the world. Been sheltered on the farm and then sheltered in Baton Rouge. I lived in a small world. Felt like I had a small personality. I thought about Guitar Slim and the way he could excite a crowd, but I didn't know whether I could do that. At the same time I knew I wanted more than what Baton Rouge had to offer. At the very least, a better job at a college in Chicago would mean more money to send home to Mama. As I tried to decide what to do, Mama stayed on my mind.

After Mama's stroke I could talk to her, but I still didn't get much reaction. I felt her spirit and I knew her love was strong as ever. Nothing could change that. But I had to do all the talking.

"Been thinking real hard," I said to her one night. She was sitting in a chair, just staring ahead. "Been thinking about going to Chicago. I know none of us ever have left you, and I'm scared to do it, Mama, but I'm also scared not to. I say that 'cause I see myself only going so far in Baton Rouge. And you know much I love that music. There's people in Chicago playing that music that I want to hear. I'm not saying I can play good as them. I can't. But just to see Muddy Waters is a dream of mine. Can't deny it. Don't wanna die, Mama, without seeing Muddy Waters. Don't wanna die without seeing Little Walter. They up there. Shorty says they play all over the city of Chicago. I'm starting to think I need to go there. But if I do, I promise you I'll make enough money to buy you a polka-dot Cadillac. How does that sound, Mama?"

Mama didn't answer, but Daddy, who'd been listening, had slipped into the room. He'd just gotten off his construction job, where he had to push wheelbarrows of concrete up and down a building site. Daddy was about the only person I know strong enough to handle that work.

"Son," he said, "if you wanna go, go. You don't need to worry about us. I told you long time ago that me and your mama ain't dying till we see all our children settled down and doing good. Now when you get to Chicago, you gonna find pretty women who gonna wanna marry you. Marry whoever you want. Makes no difference to me. Marry an elephant if you want, 'cause you the one who gotta sleep with her. Far as your work goes, remember this—I don't want you to be the best in town. I want you to be the best till the best comes around. You hear me, son?"

"I do."

I went to sleep that night and fell into crazy dreams. I was picking cotton in the dream, and then I was driving a tractor, then I was hunting in the woods with my dog, I was shooting at rabbits, when all of sudden I saw Lightnin' Slim sitting in a rocking chair playing his guitar. He was sitting under a big tree with moss coming off the branches. Maybe it's because his name is Lightnin', but right then and there the sky broke open, and a bolt of lightnin' struck his guitar and splintered it to bits. My dog started to barking, the forest caught on fire, and we had to run out of there. When I got back to the shack where I'd been raised, the shack was burning too. I was scared Mama and Daddy and my sisters and brothers were inside getting burned up, but when I turned around, they were clapping for me like I had done something great. That's when I realized I was holding a guitar and playing for my family. The fire had gone out. The storm had passed.

"Keep playing, Buddy," my mama told me in that dream. "Keep on playing."

The Day I Left Home

September 25, 1957

I think of this date like my birthday. Fact of the matter is it's my second birthday. It's when I was born again. Born this time not to stay in Louisiana, but to leave Louisiana. My life before September 25, 1957, was one thing, and my life after was something else.

I had said my goodbyes and asked Bob, Annie Mae's husband, to drive me down to Hammond, the first train stop north of New Orleans. All I had was a suitcase with a few clothes, my reel-to-reel tape with the song I cut at WXOK, and my Les Paul Gibson guitar.

"You don't got no heavy coat?" asked Bob, looking at the thin trench coat I was carrying.

"This is it," I said.

"You gonna freeze to death."

"I'll be alright," I said.

"You got not idea, boy, what's waiting for you up there."

"Ain't nobody waiting," I said. "That's what worries me."

"Don't you got Shorty's address?"

"That's all I got."

"Well, Shorty's okay. He'll see right by you. And then you saved some money, didn't you?"

"Hope I saved enough." In my pocket, hugging my thigh, was $600. Took me two years to get that money together.

When we got to Hammond, I hopped out of Bob's car and grabbed my suitcase, my tape, and my guitar. I thanked him kindly. He pulled off and then left me.

I was alone.

It was early on a Sunday morning, and that meant the train wasn't real crowded. I took a seat next to a window. I was happy and I was sad—happy to be going to a place of my dreams but sad to be leaving a family I loved. I told myself that Shorty had to be right—that I'd find the kind of job I had at LSU for better money. I told myself that with better money, life would be easier. With better money, I'd get to go to those fancy nightclubs where the curtains were red velvet and the artists—Muddy and Little Walter, Sonny Boy and Howlin' Wolf—stood on big stages and entertained everyone with their beautiful pickin' and singing. I kept the dream close to my heart: I'd see Jimmy Reed driving down the street in his limousine and he'd wave and I'd get to tell everyone back home that I done saw the great Jimmy Reed.

As the train pulled out of Hammond station, I had me some butterflies, but I was on my way.

Someone had a left a newspaper that was talking about Alaska just becoming the forty-ninth state and how Hawaii wanted to be the fiftieth. In the car in front of me a white guy had a transistor radio on a station playing "Yakety Yak" by the Coasters. I liked that song. Made me smile. Then they was playing "Catch a Falling Star," sung by Perry Como in his milky-smooth voice. Hard not to like Perry Como. Train was chugging along, and the music went with it. When the deejay put on "Get a Job," I knew I was on the right train and my smile got even bigger.

I was too excited to fall asleep. I kept looking outside, thinking that I was moving faster than I'd ever moved in my life. The speed of the train was a thrilling speed. The trees and houses and farmlands and bushes flying by were talking to me, telling me goodbye and wishing me good luck. Something good was happening.

When we pulled into Memphis in the afternoon, I was thinking about Elvis Presley because they had been playing his songs on that transistor radio. I remembered Memphis was his home. Didn't know it then, but Memphis was also the home of B. B. King and other bluesmen. If someone had told me that, I loved B. B. well enough to get off the train at Memphis and go a-searching for him. But no one told me. I just thought of Elvis Presley. By the way he sang and moved, I knew Elvis had learned a lot from bluesmen. Wasn't nothing wrong with Elvis except that he didn't concern me. Newspapers were saying he was off in the army, that he'd gone to Germany, but I didn't care. I was thinking of Chicago. After a long stopover, the train was off heading north.

Memphis was less than halfway from home to Chicago. I had a long afternoon and evening ahead of me. We had picked up more people in Memphis, where a man took the seat next to me. Dark-skinned man wearing a gray suit and blue tie. He put his suitcase in the shelf above the seat. For fear of losing them, I kept my suitcase and guitar on my lap.

Man fell asleep and I just kept staring out the window. Till then, the day had been nice, but a thunderstorm broke out as we passed through Kentucky to Indiana. Storm was fierce—jagged bolts of lightnin' and booming crackling thunder. Didn't see how a bad storm could throw this heavy train off the track, so I wasn't nervous. I was more interested in watching how a train rides through the weather. Being inside the train reminded me of being inside our shack on the farm. The sounds of a storm can be likened to the sounds of music.

Somewhere in Indiana we passed out of the storm and the sky was clear. It was already dark, and I could see the moon shining light on the countryside. Man next to me woke up. He looked over at me and stuck out his hand. I took it, shook it, and said, "I'm Buddy."

"James."

"Good to meet you, James."

"Same here, Buddy. I miss anything while I was sleeping?"

"No, sir, just a storm."

"You mean I slept through a storm?"

"Yes, sir, you sure did."

"Well, guess means I was tired. I sure will be happy to get to Chicago."

"That your home?"

"Has been for the past ten years."

"That's where I'm headed," I said.

"You coming from Memphis?"

"Louisiana."

"You fixing on moving to Chicago."

"That's the plan."

"I moved up there from Mississippi. We strange birds, ain't we?"

"How you mean?" I asked.

"When the weather gets cold, birds fly south to where it's warm. Here we is, going from south to north. We doing it backwards."

"Haven't thought about it that way," I said, "but you right."

"I see you got a guitar."

"Yes, sir."

"You plan on earning your keep in Chicago playing that guitar?"

"No, sir. I play it for fun. Played at a few clubs back home, but I intend to get a custodian-type job at some school in Chicago. Was working at LSU in Baton Rouge."

"I heard of LSU. Big school. They give you a good job?"

"Job was fine," I said. "But pay was low. Looking for better pay in Chicago."

"You know anyone up there?"

"I do. A man from Baton Rouge. He gave me his address."

I pulled out the piece with Shorty's address on it. It said, "4719 Kenwood."

"You know where this is?" the man asked.

"No idea. Would you happen to know?"

"If it's where I think it is, I might be able to find it. You best get off at the same station as me. They call it Dorchester Station. From there I could help you."

"I'd be much obliged. Is everyone in Chicago nice as you?"

The man looked me in the eye and said it straight: "No, they ain't. For the most part, they cold as ice."

It was late when the train pulled into Dorchester Station. I grabbed my stuff and followed James out the train. The night was cool, but not cold.

Chicago! I thought to myself. *I'm in the great city of Chicago!*

The air smelled different than it smelled in Lettsworth or Baton Rouge. There were smells I didn't know.

"You smelling the steel mills and the slaughter houses," said James. "They be running twenty-four hours a day, seven days a week. You see shit coming out those smoke stacks night and day. You get used to it. Where you say you need to go, Buddy?"

I was holding that piece of paper with Shorty's address so tight that my fingers was hurting. If I lost that, I'd lose everything. "Kenwood," I said, "4719 Kenwood."

"We on 63rd and Dorchester now. That's down around 47th. We got us a little walking to do. You don't mind walking, do you?"

"No, sir."

As I took my first steps on the concrete streets of Chicago, I could hear music in the distance. Didn't know whether it was coming from a radio, a record player, or a club. The closer we got to the sound, though, the more I knew it was live music. And suddenly I saw it—right there, across the street from where we was walking—a nightclub with the door open and the music blasting out. It was guitar music, guitar blues, and my heart started racing, my blood started boiling, and it took all I had not to run over there.

Feeling what I was feeling, James smiled and said, "Hey, I know you wanna get with the music, but you best settle in first and learn the territory. I don't know the clubs around here, and that could be a rough one."

"I been in lots of clubs back home," I said.

"They different here, Buddy. They a lot different."

As we kept walking, the stinging guitar sounds faded away, but I couldn't help but wonder whether it was Muddy Waters in there. Wouldn't it be something to tell my daddy that my first night in Chicago I heard Muddy Waters?

After a while we came up on 4719 Kenwood.

"Okay," said James. "We here. I'm gonna wish you all the best."

"Can't thank you enough for your goodness."

Just as James was leaving, though, I looked at the door to the apartment building and saw all these buttons. Didn't know what they were.

"James," I said. "Could I ask you one more favor?"

"Sure thing."

"What are these buttons?"

"They're just door bells. They're buzzers that buzz to the apartment where you want to be going. Look for your friend's name and there should be a button next to it."

"What do I do with the button?"

"You never seen a doorbell before?"

"We don't got 'em back home."

"You press it. Press the doorbell and it buzzes the man's apartment."

I felt stupid not knowing these things.

"Sorry for bothering you again, James."

"No problem, Buddy. You'll see lots of things here you ain't never seen before."

As James went off into the night, I pressed the button, not knowing what to expect. Nothing happened. Waited three or four minutes, and then I pressed it again. Still nothing. When I pressed it the third time, I kept my finger on it for a while.

"Who the fuck is down there?"

The voice came from an open window on the sixth floor.

"That you, Shorty?" I asked.

"Who you?"

"Buddy. Buddy Guy from back home."

"Buddy Guy? That really you?"

"In the flesh," I said.

"Come on in. Sixth floor. Apartment 634."

I walked in the building. Smelled like cats had pissed all over the floor. I climbed up the stairs, looking at these doors and wondering who was living behind them. Out of breath, I made it to the sixth floor. Walked down the long hallway and found 634. Opened the door, and there was Shorty in his drawers.

"Put your bags down," he said, "and use the bathroom if you wanna. It's at the end of the hall. If you need tissue paper, I got some up in that cabinet. I'm pleased to see you, Buddy, but I gotta get back to sleep. What time is it now?"

"Little after midnight."

I looked around his place. It was one room with a tiny little refrigerator, a sink, and a bed.

"Where do I sleep?" I asked Shorty

"Only got me one bed up in here. When I go off to work, you can use it. You gonna have to wait till I'm up."

"What time you get up?"

"Come back 'round 5 a.m."

"Where do I wait?"

"They got these coffee shops that stay open. Buy yourself a cup of coffee and they'll let you wait there."

"Is it safe to leave my stuff here?" I asked.

"Real safe," said Shorty. "Anyone break in here, I got my gun next to my pillow."

"Everyone got guns up here?"

"Anyone with any sense," Shorty said.

I went down the hall to use the bathroom. I saw that the light was on and someone was using it. I waited. I heard a toilet flush and then a big woman walked out the door. She looked me up and down and then went on her way. The bathroom was small. The smells were strong. I did what I had to do and left.

I walked back down the stairs and stood in front of the apartment building. Didn't know which way to turn. I was going to ask Shorty directions to the nearest coffee shop, but I could see he was tired and groggy. I'd disturbed his sleep and didn't wanna disturb him no more. So I just decided to walk until I found something. Must have walked seven or eight blocks when I saw a yellow light off in the distance coming out a store window. When I got up on it, I saw it was a little restaurant with a long counter lit by two naked light bulbs on strings hanging from the ceiling. There was a white man frying eggs on a griddle. I was hungry and wanted to eat, but I was afraid of spending too much money too soon. The place was empty except for two black women sitting in a booth. They were talking real loud, like they was excited. I sat at the counter.

"What will it be?"

"Cup of coffee, please."

"Coffee coming right up."

He poured the coffee into a cream-colored mug. I added milk and sugar. It tasted real good, real sweet. When he was through scrambling the eggs, he carried the food over to the women. They wolfed it down like they hadn't eaten in a week. When they was through eating, they got up to leave, but first they came over to me.

"You want a date?"

For a second I didn't understand, but then the light bulb went on. They was working women.

"Well?" she asked.

"No, thank you."

"Won't cost you too much, given that you young and sweet."

"Well, ma'am," I said, "I better stay put."

Up close, I could see their eyes were hard but their faces were pretty. They were ten, maybe fifteen years older than me. They were shapely. One was short with a big bosom that attracted me mightily. The other was taller. Her chest was flat, but her backside was beautiful. I couldn't help but notice her backside.

"You sure?" asked the busty one. "You could have a date with the two of us. You ever done something like that?"

"No, ma'am."

"Well, then, you must be new around here."

"I am. Just arrived."

She smiled a big smile and said, "We could welcome you to a Chicago with a party that you sure enough will never forget."

"Better not," I said. "Better just sit here with my coffee."

"What'd you say your name was?" she asked.

"Buddy. Buddy Guy."

"Alright, Mr. Buddy Guy. You go on and sit there with your coffee. But if you get lonely, we work around here all the time. We be looking for you."

"Thank you, ma'am," I said. "Thank you kindly."

After I Left Home

Shorty

Shorty turned out to be a great guy except when he got to drinking—and he got to drinking a lot. When he was all out of money, he'd sell a pint of blood at Michael Reese Hospital for $5. A pint of gin was ninety cents, so could have a good time with that blood money. Shorty liked to dance when he drank, which meant he'd ask me to play the guitar. That part was okay, but then he'd up and disappear and leave me back at his place, alone with my guitar. If I hadn't slept, I'd have a chance to rest in his bed. Rest was good, and I needed some 'cause hanging out at the all-night cafes was wearing me down. On the other hand, no one had taken me to see Muddy Waters or Little Walter or Howlin' Wolf.

I was keeping all those frustrations to myself. My shyness was still ruling my mind. I also had a fear that Shorty might turn me out, so I stayed on my best behavior. If he had company over, for example, he might say, "Buddy, you go out and buy us some whiskey." I'd do that, of course, 'cause Shorty was letting me stay at his place. I did that a lot. Didn't want nobody to get upset with me, especially Shorty.

After some weeks of me walking the streets at night until I could use Shorty's bed, I met a nice woman named Joyce. She took a liking to me and offered to show me how the busses and subways work. She took her time to explain how the city was laid out.

"You in the South Side now," she said. "South and west is black and north is white."

"How 'bout the music?" I asked. "Where do the blues guys play?"

"South Side and West Side. White folk ain't interested in no blues."

I already knew that was true in the South, so I wasn't surprised to hear it was true in Chicago too.

After riding the trains with this lady, I got bolder about going out. I could see how the city worked. The Loop was downtown, where they had all the tall buildings and department stores. Never seen nothing like that before. Never seen so many people hustling and bustling. Looked like everyone had somewhere to go and money to spend. I also saw where you could walk along the river until it emptied into the lake with the wind and the smell of fresh water in your face. I liked walking along the lake and trying to let go of my fears. It wasn't easy—my fears were deep.

In October the wind turned chilly. At the same time I felt chilly attitudes when I went asking for the kind of job I had at LSU. Took me a while to find the colleges where they might need a utility man, and when I did find the people in charge, they didn't show no interest. That got me thinking it might be better to find work at a service station. A couple of them needed tow truck drivers, but when they asked me if I knew the city I had to say no.

"Until you learn the streets around here," said one station owner, "you ain't doing me no good."

"Got a fine sense of direction," I said. "I can learn the streets in just a couple of weeks."

"Can't wait no two weeks. Need someone now."

So it was back to Shorty's, where I had to bide my time. He called his little apartment a kitchenette. Shorty's building was like hundreds of other buildings on the South Side that used to house large apartments. Seeing all these people coming up from the South, the landlords cut up those big apartments into tiny kitchenettes. That way they'd collect more rent. Before, you might have four apartments on a floor. Afterwards, on that same floor you might have twenty kitchenettes. In some kitchenettes a family of ten was packed in like sardines. This amazed me. I was used to the country, where there was enough space for everyone.

Bad as kitchenettes were, though, I wanted one of my own. Wandering around all night until Shorty went to work got old fast. Getting turned down for job after job was even more frustrating.

Because I wasn't getting anywhere looking for a regular job, I started thinking about that reel-to-reel tape I'd brought from Baton Rouge. My plan was to get work—and then go to Chess Records. I figured I'd do what I'd done in Baton Rouge: get me a regular service station–type job and then see about my music. After weeks of not finding no service station–type job, though, my plan changed. I decided to find my way to Chess Records to see if Mr. Leonard Chess would listen to the song I'd made at WXOK.

I put on my little green jacket that I wore on stage in Louisiana, and carrying my Les Paul Gibson in one hand and reel-to-tape in the other, I went to 2120 Michigan Avenue. That's where Chess had their office and studio. Naturally I was nervous—and also excited. Maybe I'd run into Muddy Waters. Given the fact that my contact at WXOK personally knew Leonard Chess and had given me a letter of introduction, hope was stirring in my heart.

Remembering all the great Muddy, Little Walter, Howlin' Wolf, Sonny Boy, and Jimmy Rogers records that came out of Chess

Records, I figured their headquarters would look like a palace. I figured wrong. It was a skinny, plain-looking building that sat between a supply company and rundown rooming house. When I opened the front door, there was a receptionist sitting behind a desk. The office was nothing to write home about.

"Can I help you?" she asked.

"Here to see Mr. Leonard Chess."

"You have an appointment?"

"No, ma'am, but I do have a tape."

"You need an appointment to see Mr. Chess."

"I understand . . . but . . . let me introduce myself. I'm Mr. Buddy Guy, and I'm from Baton Rouge. Actually, from Lettsworth, but before I came up here to Chicago I was living in Baton Rouge, where I made this tape at a radio station called WXOK. Diggy Doo, the deejay at WXOK, well, he knows Mr. Leonard Chess very well. They been doing business for years, and he thought this song I did—it's called "Baby Don't You Wanna Come Home"—is pretty good. Gotta good snap to it, and so he gave me this letter to give to Mr. Chess."

"That a Les Paul Gibson you got there?" asked a man who just walked through the door. He was carrying a guitar himself.

"Yes, sir, it is," I said.

"Ain't that something! Been looking for a guitar just like that. Lookee here, you wouldn't mind me using it for a session I'm running into right now?"

"You ain't gonna steal it, are you?"

Man smiled and extended his hand. "I'm Wayne Bennett, and no, motherfucker, I ain't gonna steal your guitar. Just need to borrow it. But you can come in and listen to the session and when it's over, take your guitar with you. Won't ever leave your sight."

"I guess that's okay, but I'm trying to get this meeting with Mr. Leonard Chess."

"Leonard's gonna be at the session. He gonna run the session. He runs everything around here. He's top dog. You can talk to him after the session's over."

"That's great," I said. "In that case, use my guitar all you like."

I followed him into the studio, where he took my guitar, plugged it into an amp, and played like it was his. The Spaniels were a doo-wop group I knew from their big hit, "Goodnight, Sweetheart, Goodnight." I was fascinated to watch them weave together their harmonies. I saw that Wayne Bennett was reading music set in front of him on a stand. He read it beautifully. I had to admire that because I couldn't—and still can't—read a note. The session happened real fast. They recorded three or four songs. Occasionally they'd get some directions from a white man in the control booth who I figured had to be Leonard Chess. Tried to get a good look at him, but I didn't have a good angle. I heard him say, "Do it again faster," and then he said, "Too fast. Slow it down." He had an idea for a guitar introduction. At one point he told Wayne to play a solo in the middle of the song.

Meanwhile, I didn't say nothing to no one. I was just a bug in the rug. When the session was over, Bennett handed me back my guitar and said, "Thanks, man. It's a good-feeling guitar."

"You think you could introduce me to Mr. Chess?" I asked.

"Sure thing."

When we got to the control room, though, Leonard Chess had walked away. He'd gone to his office. When we got to his office, the door was closed. Bennett knocked. No answer. So he knocked again. "Not now!" a voice shouted through the door.

"No can do," said Bennett. "Maybe next time. See ya around."

On the way out I stopped by the receptionist's desk and said, "Would you mind giving this tape and letter to Mr. Leonard Chess?"

"I'll try."

I never heard another word about that tape.

I don't believe Chess ever bothered listening to it. I was disappointed, but I was happy to have had the chance to hear a great guitarist like Wayne Bennett and watch the Spaniels sing in the studio.

On the way home I asked myself whether I could ever get learn to read music and find work in the studio. The answer was no. I didn't have a chance. Here in Chicago, I was out of my league. I'd do better learning the streets and finding work driving a tow truck.

708

In Chicago, winter is a bitch. Wind comes howling off the lake and freezes every blood cell in your body. You ain't experienced bone-chilling cold till you experience Chicago cold. And if you walking around for months on end, looking for a job you can't find, having one person after another tell you how you ain't qualified, it's easy to get down, easy to think back to warm Louisiana nights and Mama's home cooking. After a while your mind starts to wondering, *Do I really belong here? And how long is my little money gonna last?*

Money had been leaking outta me since I arrived. Can't say nothing bad about Shorty because without him, I would have never made the trip. The man took me in, and I'm forever grateful. But Shorty had his own life and couldn't be bothered taking me here and there to find work. In the beginning he said he would, but I understood why he didn't.

I've always been proud, even as a young man. The idea of begging or borrowing ain't never been attractive. Always wanted to do for myself. But pride don't put no food in your body, and come late winter 1958, some five or six months after I'd arrived, pride had me straight-up starving. It'd been more than two days since I'd had a square meal. I was flat broke, walking the streets of the South Side with my guitar, thinking of borrowing a dime to call my daddy in Baton Rouge for a ticket home. I was ready to swallow my pride.

Must have been about seven o'clock at night when a man stopped me on the street to say, "That your guitar?"

"Yes, sir."

"Can you play the thing?"

"Yes, sir."

"Buy you a drink if you play me some blues."

"How 'bout a hamburger?" I asked. "Ain't eaten in a while."

"No hamburger," said the guy. "Hamburger won't work."

"Why not?"

"You know anything about dogs?"

"A little."

"You give a dog a big piece of meat, and he won't hunt. But a hungry dog, well, that's another story—he'll hunt all night."

Couldn't argue with his logic, but I was still hungry as hell.

"You willing to play for a glass of wine?" he asked.

"Guess so," I said.

We went to a bar, where he bought me a glass of cheap wine. Right then and there, I picked up the guitar and sang some Jimmy Reed. Everyone around us started clapping.

"Not bad," said the man. "Come on home so my wife can hear you."

Went home with him and met the wife.

"Honey, this young man plays the hell outta Jimmy Reed. Wait till you hear him."

As I started into playing, the wife starting into smiling. She broke out a bottle of gin and gave me a taste.

"I do believe we should take him to the 708 Club," said the man. "Ain't that an idea, honey?"

"Good idea," said the wife. "Let me grab my coat."

We walked out into the night and headed over to what was known as the 708, one of the hottest blues clubs on the South Side. The place was packed. Blues clubs in those days were almost always packed. Because the steel mills and stockyards never stopped, workers were always coming off the job, wanting a stiff drink and a hard hit of the electric blues. They wanted to relax, and booze and blues helped them do just that.

That evening the booze and blues sure as hell helped me relax, 'cause after I had a drink at the 708, I was half out of my mind with hunger and high as a kite on the liquor. I looked up to see that the band, playing some mean, straight-in-your-face blues, was on a long ledge behind the bar. The main musician was playing guitar. His guitar was on fire. Man, he was something else. When I got closer, I saw that he was playing left-handed even though his guitar was made for a right-handed man. But this guy had turned the instrument upside down and was playing it backward—and playing it great! I recognized the song, "I Can't Quit You, Baby," from the radio.

"That's Otis Rush," said the wife of the man who'd brought me here.

"Hey, Otis Rush!" screamed her husband between songs. "Got me a nigger here who can kick your ass sideways."

"Do he have a guitar?" Rush shouted from the stage.

"He do indeed!"

"Well, let him come here and we'll see about him kicking my ass."

Without those drinks in me, I would never have gone up. With those drinks, though, I flew to the stage.

In those days even the greatest guitarists like Otis Rush sat down when they played. He had bandstands for his musicians with "OR" written on the stands. So when I got up there, I was scared I'd have to read some music. But when I looked at the music stands, they was empty. They was just for show. I let out a big sigh of relief.

"What you wanna play, boy?" asked Rush.

"Guitar Slim," I said.

"'Things I Used to Do'?"

"Yes, sir."

"You start," said Otis. "I'll come in behind you."

I started, but because some magic happened, Rush never did play with me on that song. He just let me go. I believe he had to let me go. I believe no force on earth could have kept me from letting go. See, the spirit of Guitar Slim entered my soul—not just the spirit, but the showmanship. I wouldn't sit down, I couldn't sit down, and after I played the opening notes I watched myself move to the edge of the stage and jump into the crowd, just as I'd seen Slim do.

People went crazy.

"Who's that wild nigger?" I heard one guy say. "Where he from?"

"Don't know," said someone else, "but he got Otis worried."

Truth of the matter was that Otis was egging me on, encouraging me to play over my head and behind my back, just the way I'd seen Slim play. I did it, and the more I did it, the louder the crowd.

Looking back at this moment in my life, I know I was possessed. Maybe I was open to being possessed because I was scared and desperate. Maybe I knew my life depended on tearing up this club until folks wouldn't forget me.

Just as I know that the Guitar Slim spirit entered me, I was also taking in other spirits. They used to call booze and wine "spirits," and those spirits sure as hell took hold of me. It was also my first time playing in front of a Chicago blues crowd—women who'd been laboring during the day and men who'd been working the mills. These people had their own spirit. They wanted to forget the pain of trucking steel and killing cows. They wanted to get happy in a hurry. They wanted music that would blast 'em into outer space, sounds that would carry them out of this mean ol' world into another world of good feeling. I felt them saying to me, *Take it up! Take it out! Go wild! Get me higher!* I heard their calls and I wanted to answer them—I wanted to give them what they wanted.

The spirits were going crazy—but crazy in a good way.

The owner of the club, a white man named Ben Gold, also felt those spirits. He saw how everyone was reacting, got on the phone, and called a man to hurry down to hear me.

That man got there in time to hear the last couple songs I played. By the time he arrived I was still floating on a cloud. I was playing over my head. I was covered with sweat and was drained and hungry, but I felt happier than I'd been since I got off the train at the Dorchester Station. I felt like I finally had my say.

Ben Gold came up to me and said, "Someone's here to see you."

"Who?"

"The Mud wants you."

At first I didn't understand Gold. In my frazzled mind I thought he said something like "Someone wants to *mug* you." Back home I'd heard about muggings in Chicago, where a thief hits you over the head and murders you for your money. I didn't have no money, but I didn't wanna get murdered.

"Don't wanna get mugged by no one," I told Gold.

"Not mugged—*the Mud*," he explained. "I'm talking about Muddy Waters. He wants to see you."

"Muddy Waters? The Hoochie-Coochie-Man Muddy Waters?" I asked.

"That's him."

"Where is he?"

"Just went out to his car. It's that red Chevy wagon."

"You sure no one's gonna mug me?" I had to ask again.

"Positive. Just go out there."

The station wagon was new and cherry red. I saw a man sitting in the backseat. I'd seen enough pictures to know that the man was Muddy Waters. My heart started hammering. I opened the door and got in. He moved over to give me room. I felt like I'd died and gone to heaven.

First thing I noticed about the Mud was his puffy cheeks set high on his face. His dark skin had a glow. His big eyes sparkled and showed me his mood. On this night his mood was happy. His hair, worked up in a doo, was shiny and piled high on his head. He was something to see.

First thing he said was "You like salami?"

"I like anything," I said.

"I see you're hungry."

"Hungry as a horse."

"Well, I got me a loaf of bread and some good salami. I'll fix you a sandwich."

"I'd be much obliged."

"Where you from?"

"Louisiana."

"They told me your name, but I done forgot it."

"Buddy Guy."

"You a farm boy?"

"Yes, sir."

He smiled. "I thought so. I know you had to be pickin' cotton before you ever picked a guitar."

"Yes, sir. Way before."

"Like me," said the Mud. "You pick cotton long enough and you never complain 'bout having to pick the guitar."

"I never would complain about pickin' the guitar."

"You won't complain none about this salami. Comes from a Jewish delicatessen where they cut it special for me. Have a taste."

He handed me a sandwich he had made himself. I wolfed it down. Never tasted anything so good.

"Don't Lightnin' Slim play down there in Louisiana? Ain't that his territory?"

"Yes, sir. He was the first I heard."

"And Eddie Jones," said the Mud. "He plays 'round Louisiana. I know you heard him."

"Don't think so."

"I heard you was playing one of his songs tonight."

"Which one is that?"

"'Things I Used to Do.'"

"That's Guitar Slim."

"Eddie Jones is his birth name."

"Never knew that."

"He got that long cord. And he likes to jump around. I see you like jumping around too."

"Just something that happened tonight. I was just about to quit Chicago."

"You don't wanna do that."

"I don't wanna be hungry."

"Well, I'm giving you this salami, ain't I?"

"Yes, sir, you are. And I wanna thank you."

As Muddy kept talking, I found myself tapping my foot to his words. He was talking alright, but it was more like he was singing. Never had met anyone who turned talking into a song.

"I got enough salami for the two of us. I bought this salami playing the blues. All I do is play the blues. Used to drive a truck, but no more. Just blues work. I know you looking for blues work. I see it in your eyes. Ain't easy out here. Ain't all that easy finding work."

"I was at Chess Records," I said, "hoping I might find something there. But then I saw how this guitarist called Wayne Bennett could read the music they set in front of him. I can't do that."

"Me neither. You don't gotta worry none about reading music. Long as you can hear it in your head, you okay. You find any kind of work at all?"

"Been looking for months and ain't found nothing."

"Well, you sure as hell found something tonight."

"I did?"

"Ben Gold ain't no fool. He gonna give you work, not outta no charity, but because he's seen how you heat up a crowd. When a crowd gets all hot and bothered, they get to drinking."

"Funny," I said, "cause tonight was the night I almost called my daddy for a ticket home."

"Tonight you found a new home."

I walked back to Shorty's place on cloud nine.

I was feeling like I'd found more than a new home. I was feeling like I'd found a new father, and his name was Muddy Waters.

Wild Little Nigger from Louisiana

In those early days I was a lost ball in high weeds. After that night at the 708, though, I started to find myself. I saw that the tough Chicago crowds might accept me. But I also saw that I had to put on a show. I just couldn't go up and do some straight pickin'. I needed an act.

No way I could compete with the guitarists of the day. I'm talkin' 'bout Earl Hooker, the greatest slide man in the history of slides. No guitarist in his right mind wanted to tangle with Earl. I'm also talkin' 'bout Otis Rush and Magic Sam and Freddie King. They was masters, they was monsters, they was killers. There never was—and never will be—another time when so many gunslinger guitarists terrorized the streets of any city. Most of them couldn't read no music, but the ones who could—Matt Murphy and Wayne Bennett—also gigged in Red Saunders's band at the Regal Theater when the big acts like Billy Eckstine or Della Reese came to town.

I was intimidated, but I was also scheming about how to get the attention I needed. For example, they had these guitar battles on Sunday afternoons in some of the different clubs. The prize was a pint of whiskey. If I just got up there and played toe to toe against Earl Hooker, Hooker would hand me my ass on a platter—I didn't have a snowball's chance in hell. But on a night when there was three feet of snow, I hooked up my 150-foot Guitar Slim–styled cord and started playing from inside a car parked outside the bar. The crowd was screaming long before they ever saw me. And when I finally did step through the door, the yelling was so loud that the owner handed me the pint.

"You done won," he said. "No one gonna get 'em screaming like you."

Week after week, against the greatest guitarists, I won that pint, though I never got to drink it 'cause Shorty was usually with me. Shorty would have the liquor all gulped down while I was still into singing my first song.

Unlike the other guitarists, I never sat down. I never started playing inside the club. No matter how cold or hot the evening, I'd come marching in, my guitar screaming. I might march into the men's room and play from there. Hell, I might march in the ladies' room and play from there. I'd jump off the bandstand and sit at some pretty woman's table if she was alone. I'd leap up on the bar and play flat on my back. I'd pick the thing with my teeth. I'd put it between my legs and stroke it all sexy. I'd wave it around the room like it was a flag. I'd do any goddamn thing to get them to like me.

Ben Gold helped by booking me back at the 708. Winning those contests also helped. In a few weeks time word was out. Folk started talkin' 'bout this wild little nigger from Louisiana. Money was still funny—I'd only got a few bucks a night and whatever tips was thrown at me—but I could eat. I could stop thinking about going back home with my tail between my legs. I could see that, for better or worse, I could deal with Chicago.

Never was easy because Chicago was a violent city. The violence wasn't drive-by like today. It was mainly violence with two cats who knew each other. They may be fighting over money, but usually they be fighting over a woman. I also saw that many of the men were like me: they came from the farms in the South to factories in the city. That's a rough change. You don't got your mama, you don't got your daddy, and you got some boss screaming at you to hit the steel harder or kill the cow quicker. You working crazy hours and, though the pay ain't bad, you working in a way you ain't ever worked before. You miss the open sky and fields of golden corn and white cotton. You miss the fresh vegetables from the garden. You ain't used to no crazy snowstorms and ice-covered streets where you fall on your ass every two or three steps. And the music, though it's great, is different.

Guitars didn't begin with no electricity. They was wood and strings. Same goes for the harmonica. Wasn't no way to amp it up. When we was young, we heard those guitars that are now known as acoustic. They were played soft because they were played in a room or on a porch where three or four or five people were gathered. Didn't need to be loud. The blues came through them in a beautiful tone—straight from the heart of the guitarist to the hearts of the folk listening. The softness of those notes did something to the soul. I'd say it soothed the soul.

Now come on up to Chicago and—Lord, have mercy—those guitars are plugged into the walls and screaming loud as sirens. The sound is coming out an amplifier. It needs to be loud because the barrooms in Chicago are loud. The folk are happy and excited to be off work, and they wanna talk and tell stories at the top of their lungs. They got energy to release. So if you a musician and wanna be heard, you gotta pump up and project. Baby, you got to shout. That shouting is a thrilling thing to behold. If you went into a Chicago barroom, say, in 1958, you'd be thrilled out of your mind. The electrical music would throw you back on your heels. I loved it so much because, though it was new music, it was also old music. It wasn't nothing more than country blues jacked up with big-city electricity.

I cottoned to the electricity because it was something I could turn up. Volume did a lot for me. If I couldn't play better than the guitarists around me, at least I could play louder. I could also play wilder. When I heard the buzzin' and the fuzz tones distorting the amps, that didn't bother me none. I figured fuzz tones and distortion added to the excitement of the sound. Didn't mind jammin' notes together in a way that wasn't proper. Notes crashing into each other was another way to get attention. I learned how to ride high on electricity.

The blues electricity got into the people. Sometimes it got them crazy. Mel's Hideaway, at Roosevelt and Loomis over on the West Side, was a down and dirty club that catered to the rowdy crowd. I played there along with almost every blues picker in Chicago. Freddie King made it famous with the "Hideaway" hit that he borrowed from Hound Dog Taylor, the bottleneck guitarist who used it as his theme song. When it came out in the early sixties, "Hideway" pushed Freddie ahead of the rest of us. Made Freddie a star.

Back in the fifties only the blues-loving crowd knew about the Hideway. Going in, you understood that almost every man was carrying a knife, gun, or razor. The women were also known to carry weapons. The women would cut you quick as the men. The men and the women would be out there grinding up on each other during a slow dance or hollering about being two-timed. You never knew. Being the cautious type, at the first pop of a gunshot I hit the floor. Fortunately, I missed the worst moment at the Hideaway. A waiter who worked there told me the story.

Waiter said, "Man walked and sat at the bar. Bartender said, 'What it'll be?'

"'Two beers and two Scotch chasers.'

"'You drinking hard,' said the bartender.

"'Need to. Feeling down.'

"'Big trouble?' asked the bartender.

"'Wife troubles,' said the man.

"'Those the kinda troubles that can get you down.'

"'Not anymore.'

"The man threw back the beers, threw back the Scotches, and ordered two more. Bartender gave him new drinks and asked, 'How did you solve your troubles?'

"Man said, 'I got the answer right here in this paper bag.'

"Man put a paper bag on the bar.

"'How could a paper bag solve your wife problem?' asked the bartender.

"'Go on and look inside,' said the man.

"Bartender put his hand in the paper bag and felt something hairy.

"'Pull it out,' said the man.

"Bartender pulls it out and right there, in his hand, is the bloody, cut-off head of a woman.

"'Motherfucker!' the bartender screamed.

"'Told you I done solved the problem,' said the man.

By then, though, the bartender had run out of Mel's Hideway, never to be seen again.

At the Squeeze Club, also called the Bucket of Blood—every big city had a rough bar nicknamed Bucket of Blood—I was playing my guitar when one cat drove an ice pick deep into another cat's neck. That way you bleed on the inside and there ain't no mess. When the cat fell to the ground, they dragged him outside and dumped him on the corner. Seeing all this, I got sick to my stomach.

When the cops saw the dead man, they couldn't have cared less. Didn't even investigate. To them it meant only one more dead nigger. In those days cops came around for their bribes and nothing else. If the cops ever pulled you over while you was driving, you just handed 'em five bucks. They didn't even wanna see no driver's license. Too much trouble.

Then there were enforcers, big guys who worked for the club owners. They'd throw you out if you was raising too much hell. A guy was thrown out of the Sealy Club on Madison. That burned him up so bad, though, that he came back with a gallon of gasoline, poured it all over the front door, and lit the joint on fire. Several people burned to death. In those days there weren't no laws about safety exits.

There was one exit I didn't think I'd ever make. This happened back at the Squeeze. Didn't know a soul at the time. I'd played a couple of songs, and a customer bought me a Schlitz beer. Man come up to me and said, "Nigger, the way you looking at my woman, I should cut your dick off."

Naturally those are not friendly words. Right away I knew I was in trouble. In truth, I didn't even know who his woman was.

"You got me mixed up with someone else," I said. "I ain't looked at your woman."

"Don't lie to me, nigger. You up playing your fancy guitar and you eyeing my woman. You 'bout to get cut."

I thought fast and said, "Just to show you how I'm feeling, I'm telling you that not only am I not wanting your woman, I'm gonna give you mine. That way you'll have two women."

"Say what?"

"I'll say it again. Keep your woman and take mine."

Man looked confused, thought it over, and then started to laugh.

"Never have been offered another man's woman," he said. "You all right. I'm buying you a beer."

He bought me a beer and left me alone. I was relieved that he didn't ask for my woman, 'cause I didn't have none.

For my first years in Chicago I didn't mess with no women because even if they would give me a tumble, I had nowhere to do the tumbling. I couldn't count on Shorty's place because there was no telling when he'd be coming and going. Didn't have no money for a boarding room or a bed in a motel. Women were a luxury I couldn't begin to afford.

The 708 was my first home base. That was where Muddy would come look after me. He kept feeding me that salami and telling me I could play the guitar. He'd just sit there and smile while I played. That smile was better than the few dollars Ben Gold was giving me.

One night in late '58 B. B. King showed up at the 708. I was so nervous playing in front of him that my hands were trembling. I would have jumped off a building to see B. B., but here he was, coming to see me. Muddy was twenty-three years older than me, and like I said, I looked on him like a father. B. B. is eleven years older, and he was more like a big brother. B. B. is not a rough character like many of the bluesmen. He has a gentle soul and sweet heart. He don't do no bragging like the other guitar gunslingers. That night when I met him he couldn't have been nicer.

"People been saying you sound like me, so I had to come in here and listen for myself," he said.

"B. B.," I said, "I ain't good enough to sound like you."

"Well, you sounding good. All I can tell you is this—use straight picks when you play. You gonna have less trouble with straight picks."

Lightnin' Hopkins used finger picks—the kind that actually attach to your fingers—while straight picks (also called flat picks) are those you hold between your thumb and index finger. Well, I took B. B.'s advice, and I use straight picks to this day.

"B. B.," I said, "I noticed that you never use a slide."

"Never learned how. Now my cousin, Bukka White, I met up with him when I got to Memphis. Bukka had that bottleneck. He'd slide it over his fat fingers and, man, he'd make the prettiest sound you ever did hear. If he wanted to get even slicker, he'd use a pipe. Well, I'm telling you, Buddy, when he wasn't looking, I'd try it myself. I wanted that pretty sound, but I just couldn't do it. Couldn't work the slide no how. All I could was bend the strings. That got me a crying sound, but you got that sound too."

"Copied from you," I admitted.

"Hell, I was trying to copy T-Bone Walker and Lonnie Johnson and all the others who got there before me. I wasn't good enough to sound like them, so I stumbled on something that sounds like me."

From there we got to talking about the farm. Turned out he was raised as a sharecropper in Mississippi. When B. B. was a kid, he was picking cotton and riding the mule, like I had.

"You're a good one," he said. "If I can help you, just let me know."

Some of the guitar gunslingers wouldn't help you if you was bleeding to death. They'd see that as one less competitor to worry 'bout. But others, like B. B. and Muddy, couldn't do enough for you. God blessed them with a generous spirit. Those are the guys I was trying to be like.

You can read books that say there was a South Side style to the Chicago blues and then a West Side style, but I say that's bullshit. We was playing all over. I started out at the 708 on the South Side, but I went to the Squeeze Club on the West Side.

Muddy told me before he ever played regularly in clubs that he and Walter and them would set up on Maxwell Street in Jewtown—this is on the Near West Side—where pushcarts were selling everything from lima beans to lime-green trousers.

"It happened on the weekends," said the Mud. "You'd get over there around noon to find you a spot on the street. You just started playing. If it rained, you stuck an umbrella over your head and played again. Could be snowing, could be sticky hot—didn't make no difference 'cause the people, they'd come no matter what. They shopping for junk and jewelry and God knows what. Everyone looking for a bargain. You ain't ever seen so many people out there as there was on Maxwell Street. You'd make good money on Maxwell Street. I liked it a lot better than being up in these clubs with the guys pulling out their knives and shooting off their pistols. Ain't no more music on Maxwell Street these days, but if you wanna good suit at a cheap price, go down to Jewtown, Buddy, and tell 'em Muddy sent you."

When I asked the Mud whether it was better playing on the South Side or the West Side, he laughed and said, "You'd best be playing on every side. Don't make no difference. Long as they pay."

When I arrived five minutes late at one West Side Club, the owner said he wouldn't pay.

"You said you'd be here at 9 p.m.," the owner told me.

"Took the wrong train," I explained. "It's barely past the hour anyway."

"I ain't paying."

I wasn't about to go back to Shorty's, so I walked past him into the club, plugged my guitar into my amp, jacked up the volume, jumped on top of the pool table, and started into pickin'. Crowd went nuts. Man said, "No matter, I still ain't paying you." Didn't argue 'cause the tips were good enough to keep me going.

The other thing that kept me going was getting to see the bluesmen I'd always dreamed of seeing.

One night I was dead asleep at Shorty's. He was shacked up with some woman, so I had the place to myself for a night or two. Good chance to catch up on my sleep. Must have been three in the morning when a knock on the door woke me up. It was Joyce, the lady who'd shown me how the buses and trains worked.

"Buddy," she said, "hate to wake you, but I remember you saying how you'd give anything to see Jimmy Reed. Well, a friend of mine just got back from Pepper's where Jimmy's playing with his whole band."

That's all I needed to hear. I jumped out the bed, threw on some clothes, and ran over to Pepper's on 43rd Street. Must have been a helluva night, because people was laid out on the street, drunk on the music or just plain worn out from dancing. Had to step over one guy just to get in the front door.

"Jimmy Reed here tonight?" I asked the bartender.

"Was here. But they through playing."

"I'd just like to meet him. I'd just like to see him."

"You just did."

"How's that?" I asked.

"When you was walking into the club, that was the man you stepped over."

I went back out to get me a good look. Bartender was right. Jimmy Reed was passed out cold in front of Pepper's, his face in the gutter, his red felt fedora all crushed up against his head.

One Whole Chicken

I'd heard Magic Sam, another gunslinger, playing around town. He had seen me win a bunch of those Sunday afternoon guitar-cutting contests. After I had won my fourth pint of whiskey in a row, he came up to me and asked, "You ever been in the studio?"

"One time back home at a radio station. Cut me a song."

"Anything happen with it?"

"I put it on tape and gave it to Leonard Chess."

"Chess like it?"

"Don't think he ever heard it."

"Sounds like Leonard Chess. He don't listen to nothing except what Willie Dixon gives him."

"Who's Willie Dixon?"

"Bass player. Songwriter. Or at least a guy who knows how to put his name on a song, whether he wrote it or someone else did. Worked for Leonard for years."

"Maybe he can help me."

"I can help you, Buddy," said Sam. "That's why I'm here. Willie Dixon and Leonard Chess done fell out. Willie be working with Eli Toscano, the guy who puts out my stuff."

"At Cobra Records?"

"Eli owns Cobra. I want you to meet him. Want you to meet Willie too."

I tried to figure out Magic Sam's angle. I couldn't. Turned out he didn't have none. Just wanted to help.

I was excited 'cause I knew Cobra was where Otis Rush made "I Can't Quit You, Baby." Magic Sam was cutting sides over there along with Harold Burrage and Betty Everett. I'd hear those songs on the radio—and that was good enough for me. Cobra wasn't Chess, but no one was taking me to Chess, and now all of sudden Magic Sam was taking me to Cobra.

The operation was on Roosevelt Road on the West Side, which was why you had folks talkin' 'bout the West Side blues style of Magic and Otis. Toscano had a little record store with a garage in the back. The garage was the studio. Behind the counter at the store was a man I recognized from posters around town.

"Ain't you Harold Burrage?" I asked.

"That's me."

"You selling records here?"

"Sure am. Wanna buy some? Got my own records for sale."

"I'm supposed to meet Magic Sam."

"Why?"

"He wanted me to meet Eli."

"To make a record?"

"I guess."

"Eli don't record just anybody."

Sam walked through the door just in time to say, "This cat ain't just anybody. He's Buddy Guy. He plays guitar and sings."

"We got enough guitarists and singers 'round here," said Burrage, a good singer himself.

"Not like this. Where's Eli?"

"Where he always is—in the back shooting craps."

Sam walked behind curtains. I heard voices, and in a little while Eli Toscano came out. He was a short man with a foreign accent. Never did learn where he came from originally. He was very direct.

"Play something," he said.

I broke into B. B. King's "Sweet Sixteen" so strong that Burrage practically jumped over the counter and told Toscano, "Give this motherfucker a contract. Now!"

"He gotta talk to Willie first," said Toscano. "I'm not doing anything unless Willie wants to do it."

Willie Dixon took me to a big barbecue restaurant where he ordered a whole chicken. I figured that was for him and me to share, so I didn't order nothing. But when the platter arrived, he took the entire bird in his hands and started tearing into it. I mean, he devoured the whole chicken in nothing flat. Didn't offer me a single bite. But that was okay. I wasn't there 'cause I cared about eating but 'cause I wanted to make a record. Later, though, I'd learn that Willie would devour songwriting credits just like he devoured that chicken.

Willie was a big man, about twenty years older than me. Must have weighed three hundred pounds, but it was mainly muscle, not fat. He was a talker. When I'm with a man like this, the more he talks, the more I shut up. According to Willie, he'd done everything and knew everyone. He came up from Mississippi, where he saw the KKK take a black man, bury him up to his neck in the ground, and then sic the dogs on him. He described how the dogs fed on his face until he was dead. Then he talked about coming to Chicago and making all these records in the forties with famous people, and how without him no one would have heard of Chess.

"How come you ain't there now?" I asked.

"Money, son," he said. "It's always about money. Leonard wasn't giving me my due. Was also interfering too much with how I make the records. Toscano's letting let me do it the way *I* wanna do it—the way it should be done. You heard 'I Can't Quit You, Baby'?"

"Everyone's heard that."

"That's my song, my arrangement, my production."

I didn't even know what the word "production" meant, but I wasn't about to ask.

"You like Otis Rush?" Dixon asked me.

"He's great."

"I'll get him to play on your record."

"Oh, man," I said, "if you get him, you won't need me."

"We'll get him to play in the background. I like two guitars on a song. Y'all can harmonize."

"I don't know how."

"I'll show you. I'll show you everything."

"What song am I gonna sing?"

"I got lots of songs."

"I got some ideas of my own," I said.

"I wanna hear them, Buddy. Maybe I can do something with them."

"How much I get paid?"

"You worried about money, son, or you worried making a record?"

"I wanna make a record, but didn't you say it's always about money."

"I'll take care of you, Buddy. You just take care to be on time."

"When do we start?"

"Gimme a few weeks."

In those weeks I went looking for new clubs where I could play. The competition was so keen that, even after I did okay at one spot, someone might come behind me and draw a bigger crowd. Then the owner would get off me and on him.

There was as many jazz clubs in Chicago as blues clubs, and some of the cats told me I could handle a jazz gig if I learned to fake the chords and play songs like "Flying Home" and "Little Red Top." I loved jazz and appreciated all that the jazz guitarists were doing. T-Bone had jazz flavor to his blues; Matt Murphy and Wayne Bennett could work their way through any jazz song. They were wizards, but I wasn't. I could barely get through a jazz set. I spent most of the time fumbling.

One night Earl Hooker heard what I was doing. "You trying to play shit you don't know how to play," he said. "I don't know how to play it either."

"You don't?"

"I don't wanna know. It confuses my brain. Blues is good enough for me. Don't go off in too many different directions. Just go in one. Stick to the blues clubs, baby."

Theresa's, down in a basement at 48th and Indiana, was one of the biggest clubs on the South Side. I wanted to play there, and one night I showed up hoping that the owner, Theresa Needham, had heard of me.

"Not only have I heard of you," she said, "but I heard you played here last night and you wasn't shit. You can't play worth a damn."

"Last night? I wasn't here last night."

"The hell you wasn't. I know one nigger from another, and your black ass was here last night playing some sorry shit. Folks ran outta here swearing they'd never come back. I told *you* never to come back."

"Must have been someone else?"

"You arguin' with me?"

Wasn't sure what to say next. Theresa was a sight to behold: a mean-looking lady wearing a dirty apron with two pockets. In one was a pistol, in the other a billy club. Theresa was no one to fuck with.

"Begging your pardon, ma'am," I said meekly, "but with all due respect I ain't ever set foot in your club. Maybe there's someone who looks like me or is going around using my name, but he ain't me. If you let me play one song tonight, I do believe I can make my point directly."

"One song, nigger, and then you out."

"You mind if I start playing from out on the street?"

"Don't got any more time to fool with you. Just play and be gone."

I hooked up my 150-foot cord and started from outside the club. I went back into my Guitar-Slim bag of tricks, turned my amp so loud that dogs started barking, and gave it all I got, beginning with Bobby Blue Bland's "Further on Up the Road."

"Goddamn," said Theresa, seeing the customers go crazy for my act, "why didn't you play that shit last night?"

"I keep saying, ma'am, that wasn't me last night."

"Well, I want you in here tonight, and tomorrow night too."

From then on people packed her club to see me until Theresa became my biggest fan. With that steady work, I figured I could afford to move out of Shorty's into a place of my own.

Found me a kitchenette at 4625 Lake Park on the South Side, not far from Muddy. It was tiny, but all them apartments were tiny. I was just grateful to have a bed of my own. No more waiting around for Shorty to get up and go out. It was a luxury—sleeping whenever the hell I felt like it.

Weekend before the Cobra session, I was playing a gig at Mitch's Jukebox Lounge. Joint was jammed. During the break I had to go to the bathroom. I kept my guitar on the bandstand under the watchful eye of the club owner, Jimmy Mitchell. When I got back, the guitar was gone. My heart dropped to the floor.

"Jimmy!" I cried. "What happened to my guitar, man?"

"Nothing to worry 'bout, Buddy. All under control."

"What you mean under control? I'm missing my guitar."

"Your valet took it."

"My valet. You know me, Jimmy. You know I don't got no valet."

"He called himself your valet."

"He was lying. Which way he go?"

"Out the back door."

I ran, but the back alley was empty. My "valet" was long gone, along with my Gibson Les Paul.

This was on a Saturday. The Cobra session was Monday—no guitar, no record. What the hell was I gonna do?

I had only one idea. It meant eating my pride, but sometimes that's what you gotta do.

Sunday afternoon I headed over to Theresa's, where the boss was back in the kitchen, wearing her apron with the pistol and billy club sticking out.

"What the fuck you doing here so early? Go home and rest up for tonight."

I started stammering. "I . . . I . . ."

"Boy," she said, "what you want?"

"They stole my guitar."

"They did what?"

"They stole my Gibson."

"How the hell they do that?"

"Cat told Jimmy Mitchell he was my valet and ran off with it."

"Jimmy Mitchell is one ignorant motherfucker. What you gonna do now?"

"Don't know."

"Doesn't Mitchell know that your guitar is your bread and butter? You should get him to buy you one."

"He won't."

"Figures. He's a cheap bastard."

"I'm in a jam," I said. "Got me a recording date Monday and no guitar."

"You got money to buy another one?"

"No, ma'am."

"Now wait a minute, boy. You couldn't be here expecting I'd give you that money?"

"No, ma'am."

"Then why you here?" she asked, her hands on her hips.

"Thought maybe I could borrow the money."

"Borrow how much?"

"Figure a Strat could cost $160."

"What the hell is a Strat?"

"The kinda guitar Guitar Slim plays."

"So Buddy Guy, thinking he's as good as Guitar Slim, wants to buy him a fancy guitar."

"Well, ma'am . . ."

"Don't 'well' me. Just come take this fuckin' money and pay me back soon as you can. I figure the way you been playin', you gonna wind up richer than all of us."

Next thing I knew, she reached deep into her brasserie and fished out $160.

Cobra Records, here I come.

A Copyright? What's a Copyright?

Before I went over to Toscano's record store I went around to Theresa and gave her a dollar.

"What the hell is that?" she asked.

"Guitar cost $159. You gave me $160."

She laughed out loud and said, "Boy, you crazy. I don't need no dollar."

"It's yours, ma'am, not mine."

"Let me see you new guitar."

I showed her my sunburst Fender Stratocaster, fresh out the music store.

"Mighty pretty," she said. "By the twinkle in your eye, I do believe you love that guitar more than you love any female."

"Gonna pay you back if it's the last thing I do."

"Go on, Buddy, and make that record. I expect to be hearing it on the radio."

When I got to Toscano's, Willie took me back to the garage where they had hooked up a little studio. Eli Toscano did the engineering. Looking back, the equipment was real raw and simple, but to me it was beautiful. There was two microphones, one for my singing and my guitar, and the other for everyone else—Willie Dixon on bass, Otis Rush on back-up guitar, Odie Payne on drums, Harold Burrage on piano, and McKinley Eaton on baritone sax.

"What am I going to sing?" I asked.

"Well, Buddy, how you feelin'?" asked Willie, who was chewing on a meaty rib dripping with barbecue sauce.

"I'm so nervous," I said, "I could sit and cry."

"Good start," said Willie. "We'll call it 'Sit and Cry.' You just start and play some blues."

"That's it?" I asked.

"Don't worry none. Just start playing some blues. We'll fill in behind you."

I sang some stuff that just came to my mind, and when I was stuck for words Willie gave me some of his own. There was no musical notes on paper, nothing written down. We did a couple of takes. The technology didn't let us do no overdubs or nothing fancy. All them horns behind me felt great. Never had no horns behind me before. When we got through, Willie said, "Sounds good, Buddy. That's gonna be a good copyright."

"Copyright," I said. "What's a copyright?"

"You don't gotta worry about that none," Willie answered. "That's just paperwork. I take care of all the paperwork for you."

"Thanks, man," I said, figuring Willie was doing me a favor.

We needed something for the flip side of the record, and Eli Toscano came up with the idea.

"You know how big Otis's 'I Can't Quit You, Baby' is?" he asked.

"Real big," I said.

"Let's cut an 'answer record.' Answer records can be big."

"What's an 'answer record'?" I asked.

"It's like when they did 'Annie Had a Baby' after 'Work with Me, Annie,'" said Willie. "One records plays off the other."

"Let's call your answer to Otis 'Try to Quit You, Baby,'" said Eli. "That'll have everyone thinking of Otis."

"Long as Otis don't mind," I said.

"Long as I get paid for this session," said Otis. "I don't give a shit."

Willie used two sax players—Harold Ashby and Bob Neely—to get a fatter sounds. Me, Eli, and Willie made up the words. Playing in front of all those instruments made me feel like B. B. King playing in front of his band. When we listened back, I was all smiles.

"Another good copyright," said Willie.

"Will they play it on the radio?" I asked. "Will they play it on WXOK so my mama can hear it down in Baton Rouge?"

"Most probably," said Willie, busy filling out copyright forms.

A couple weeks passed before I got the call to go back to the studio. Toscano wanted to cut two more songs.

When I arrived, walking through the record store to the room behind the curtains, Eli Toscano was playing poker with three guys. I had seen one of the men that day at Chess when Wayne Bennett borrowed my guitar. I recognized him as Leonard Chess, and naturally I wanted to ask him if he ever heard my tape, but I was too shy. Besides, I didn't need that tape. I was making records of my own.

"Fuck," Eli was saying, throwing down his cards. "That puts me ten Gs in the hole."

Willie Dixon had just walked in, so I could ask him, "What does ten Gs mean?"

"That's ten thousand dollars, son."

"You mean Eli Toscano lost ten thousand dollars playing cards?"

"That ain't nothing. He's lost a lot more than that."

"Good God," was all I could say.

"We got us another producer coming in today," said Willie.

"What's a producer?" I asked.

"The guy who puts together the session. Last time I was your producer. This time we bringing in Ike Turner."

"The guy who did Jackie Brenston's 'Rocket 88'?"

"So you heard of him."

"Muddy was talking about him the other day."

"You'll like him," said Willie. "He's from Mississippi like me. He's bringing Jackie Brenston with him."

"Wow," I said. "Hope I can please him."

"All you gotta do is listen to what he says."

A half-hour later Ike Turner, with a mile-high 'do atop his head, was saying, "Willie, listen to what I'm saying. Your bass is out of tune."

Willie wasn't having none of that.

"Hold up, Ike," he said. "I know how to tune a bass."

"Your bass ain't going right with the horns. Your bass is off."

I was hearing what Ike was hearing. I couldn't put it into words—I hadn't even learned the word "tuning"—but I knew Willie wasn't matching the sound of his bass with what me and Ike were playing.

Ike, by the way, had him a Strat. That made me feel like I had really chosen the right instrument.

"I took up guitar," he said to me, "'cause of Earl Hooker. You know Earl Hooker?"

"I do," I said.

"He got his shit from Robert Nighthawk. You heard him?"

"Not yet. I wanna."

"How about Gatemouth? You heard Gatemouth? You gotta love it when Gatemouth does . . . "

And with that Ike broke into "Okie Dokie Stomp," Gatemouth's big instrumental hit. He played the thing note for note.

You had to like Ike Turner. He knew his music and didn't mind showing you a thing or two. He wasn't stingy about his compliments. He told me I could play good and had me do one of his songs, "This Is the End." Though he couldn't read music, he knew how to arrange all the instruments by singing the notes. He also played piano and just about any other instrument you threw at him.

"I believe you got you a smash hit," he said when we was through.

The second song we cut, "You Sure Can't Do," felt a lot like Guitar Slim's "The Things You Used to Do."

"You said you love Slim," said Ike, "so here's your chance to tell him how much. I think it's another hit."

I laughed and sang the song. My main attitude was just to keep everybody happy and get these records out on the street. If Ike said these were hits, I wasn't about to argue.

They didn't play at the session, but Lafayette Leake and Little Brother Montgomery were around, two of the best blues piano players in Chicago. Later Little Brother would write me a hot song, but for now they was happy just to hang out and watch the great Ike Turner. It was a beautiful day.

Got even more beautiful when Eli Toscano said, "I like what you did so well that I'm starting a new label for you."

"Great," I said, not exactly sure what that meant but knowing it had to be something good.

"Magic, Otis, Harold, and Betty," he explained, "they all on Cobra. But I want the radio jocks and the public to take special note of you, Buddy. You're a real artist, so I'm starting up the Artistic label just for you."

"Thank you kindly," I said.

"I think we're going to make real money together."

If you ask me today how much I made from Toscano, I'd have to tell you not even my carfare home–not a nickel.

Far as those songs being hits, well, they got played on the radio in Chicago every once in a while—and naturally that was a thrill—but my folks didn't hear them down in Baton Rouge, and that was a disappointment. In my twenty-two-year-old mind, I saw Eli Toscano turning me into a big recording star, but that dream ended a year later when Eli was found at the bottom of Lake Michigan. Some said it was a boat accident. Some said it was bad debt from his crap shooting and poker playing. Some said he'd been hooked up with the mob ever since he went into the record business. Others said that the body wasn't Eli at all and that he was hiding out somewhere in Indiana until the heat blew over. Whatever it was, Toscano never showed up again. He was gone, Cobra was gone, Artistic was gone, and I got my first taste of what it meant to be a bluesman in the record business.

Wouldn't be my last.

Night Shift

Was I discouraged by what happened at Cobra? I'd have to say no. I was just a guitar-playing fool, happy to be making a few dollars singing my blues while building up a reputation in a town of killer gunslingers. I remember asking Muddy why John Lee Hooker didn't stay in Chicago.

"When Johnny came through," said the Mud, "he cut something for Chess called 'Walkin' the Boogie.' But then when he looked around and saw all the guitar men 'round here, he boogied on back to Detroit. Johnny didn't wanna be around all these heavy-hitters."

That made me say, "Maybe I should go to Detroit."

"Oh, no, son, you doin' right here. Matter of fact, the Wolf was asking about you. He done heard you can play."

"Where's he playing?"

"Silvio's. I don't like waking up early, but if you really wanna hear something, get there when the night shift from the slaughter house gets off. That's when the Wolf really starts to howl."

"What time is that?"

"He says the best tips come in around 7 a.m. Everyone's happy 'cause they through working. They ready to start drinking. Friday morning, when they get those paychecks, that's when it really gets to moving."

"I'm going."

"But if Wolf asks you up there to play, be careful. Play, but don't play too much. He don't like no one to outshine him. And if you outshine him too much, he don't mind punching you upside your head. You know that song he sings called 'Evil'?"

"I've heard it."

"Well, that's the Wolf. Willie Dixon says *he* wrote it. Maybe, but Wolf, he done lived it."

I got to Silvio's just as all-night workers were coming through the door. They were ready. I was ready. Howlin' Wolf was already up there, and just as night was turning to day, he was singing a song called "Break of Day."

He was sitting down while he was singing, but that didn't keep him from singing strong. After he did "Moaning at Midnight," he stopped singing and started saying, "I know you been working since midnight, and that means you been moaning since midnight, and that means you tired of hearing me moaning, so I'm gonna shut up and give you something you can smoke. Gonna give you some of this here 'Smokestack Lightnin'."

"Smokestack Lightnin'," one of Wolf's famous songs, got wild. You ain't lived until you come to a club in Chicago fresh in the morning with everyone high on hard whiskey and heavy blues. The men are ready to let off steam. The women are as wild as the men, women who ain't shy about drinking and showing you that good meat rolling over their bones. Some of them women wanna dance with you and some wanna take you home. Some love the music and some love the musicians. But just about everyone is feeling that life may be hard, but life's a helluva lot easier when the blues is blasting with Howlin' Wolf telling you that he's "Sitting On Top of the World," 'cause, baby, he sure is.

Seeing I brought my guitar that morning, Wolf asked me up to play. Wolf's regular guitarist, Hubert Sumlin, is the one of the best, so I wasn't gonna play too much, especially in light of what Muddy said. I played to highlight Wolf, not draw attention to me, and that made Wolf real happy. He let me stay on stage.

During the break Hubert took me aside. "Hey, man," he said. "if the Wolf wants to take you on the road, it's okay with me."

"I ain't interested in taking no man's gig," I said.

"I'm tired of how he gets drunk and mean. If he don't think I'm playing right, he'll try to beat up on me like I'm one of his women."

I looked over at Wolf. He was a giant of man. Wasn't no one I wanted to fight.

A week later Wolf came to hear me at Theresa's.

"You ain't half bad," he said after the set, "and I'm fed up with these motherfuckers in my band. You wanna go on the road with me?"

I thought about how much I loved this man's music. And then I thought about my health.

"No, thank you, sir," I said. "I got some gigs coming up here in town."

My first out-of-Illinois gig was down the road in Gary, Indiana. It's only twenty-five miles away on a tollway where you could drop in a bottle-top and the pay-gate would think it's a dime. After Pittsburgh, Gary was the second-biggest steel-mill city in America. In the fifties Gary was working twenty-four/seven. Far as gambling, liquor, and women went, it was wide open. You'd see cats shooting craps and playing blackjack everywhere. Cops couldn't care less. Once they got their payoffs, they'd go nap in their squad cars.

Strange to say, but women weren't allowed to sit at the bar and order a drink. They'd have to be seated at tables. But if you was riding around in your car and stopped at a light, damn if a woman wouldn't try to jump in and get you to fuck her for a few bucks.

I found a home at a club owned by two brothers, Fred and Jay. They had the F&J Lounge that sat on the corner of 15th and Adams in the heart of Gary's party district. It was bigger than any blues club in Chicago. I'd say it held 150. I'd mainly work there weekends, when, in two nights, I could make as much as $60, more than a whole week's work at Theresa's or the 708.

I'd started with a band that included Harold Burrage on piano, Jack Myers on bass, and Fred Below, the best shuffle drummer since the shuffle began. I also took two horns and a guy who danced with a Cobra to remind everyone to buy our songs on Cobra Records. I did my usual bit of starting out playing on the street and slowly working my way inside.

Gary loved blues as much as Chicago, and if anything, they were wilder with the feeling. I got so popular that the gig became regular. Even B. B. came in one night to hear what all the commotion was about.

I slipped into a routine that the owners really liked: I got the Mud and the Wolf and even Little Walter to come out and play late sets. They'd do three or four songs with my band, I'd slip them a ten, and they'd jump in their car to go back to Silvio's or Mitch's Jukebox Lounge for their regular gigs. That way Gary got the best of Chicago.

We got paid at the end of the night. Brother Fred, one of the owners, had this talent for reaching into the front pocket of his shirt and fishing out exactly the amount he owed, whether it was three tens or two twenties. This one time, though, he went to pocket, fished out the bills and, when he handed them to me, said, "I got something extra for you." He did the same thing with Harold Burrage.

We figured he was giving us an extra dollar, just to show appreciation, but when we looked at our bills they said "$1,000." I counted those zeroes at least four times and every time came up with three. A thousand dollars. Never had seen a thousand-dollar bill in my life. It was like seeing a woman with two heads or a cat with two tails. Didn't know what to make of it. Harold had the same reaction.

Fred smiled. "Ain't from me. It's from"—and here I'm gonna make up a name—"Wanda."

"Who's Wanda?" I asked. "And why she giving us this money?"

"Wanda's one of the best workers in Gary," said Fred. "One of the prettiest. She looking for some guys to take of care of her, and y'all got chosen."

"I ain't sure what that means," I said.

"Me either," said Harold, who was also not real wise in the ways of street women.

"Means be here tomorrow," said Fred.

"Tomorrow's Sunday," I said. "Indiana's dry on Sunday."

"F&J is a private club on Sunday. Invitation only. Y'all are invited."

Come Sunday Harold and I drove back to Gary. We wearing our $30 suits and curious as all get-out about what's gonna happen. F&J was locked up, but when we knocked on the door Fred was right there.

"Gents," he said, "the rest of the committee is here."

"Committee?" I asked.

"Just come on in and have a seat."

A big table had been set up in the middle of the club. Eight pimps were sitting there. Their suits had to cost $100. Next to them were twelve or thirteen fine-looking females. Some of them had long legs and skirts hoisted up high. Some of them had big beautiful breasts practically busting through their blouses. Some of them were on the plump side, but pleasingly plump. None of 'em was even close to ugly.

Wanda, the prettiest of all them, with jet-black skin and blazing brown eyes, came over to me and Harold. She let us know we were the ones.

The pimps ordered lots of liquor and a ton of food. The whores sent out for a special cake. The check was piling up. I tapped Harold on the shoulder and signaled for him to meet me in the men's room.

"What the hell's happening?" I asked. "What we doing here?"

"We eatin' with a gang of pimps and whores, that's what we doing. Liquor's good and so is the food."

"Who's paying for all this?" I asked.

"Wouldn't know."

"Maybe that's why Wanda done gave this money. Maybe we supposed to pay."

"Maybe."

"You think we should?"

"I ain't thinking," said Harold. "I'm just feeling like I died and gone to pussy heaven. You do the thinking."

"I'm gonna pick up the tab," I said.

"Good, man. You do that."

We went back to the table, and when the check came, I saw it was nearly $300. Never saw a check that big before. But I had my thousand-dollar bill. I pulled it out and laid it on the table. Next thing I knew Wanda was slapping me across the face.

"Nigger!" he screamed. "You green as a pool table and twice as square. Daddy never pays for his baby's meal. Baby takes care of Daddy."

She stuffed the thousand back in my pocket and brought out her own money. There was no arguing with Wanda.

At the end of the evening she invited me and Harold back to her house. Turned out she had three little kids.

"I know you guys are new at this," she said, "but that's why I want you. All the other Big Daddies 'round here be robbing and thieving their women. You two don't look like no robbers or thieves to me."

"No, ma'am," I assured her. "But neither is we good at the kind of work you want. We just musicians."

"But you know how to protect a woman."

"Wouldn't want no one to harm you, that's true," I said.

"And you know how to get a woman out of a jail."

"That just takes money."

"I got the money," said Wanda, pointing to her purse.

"Well, then, you don't need no one to do what you can do yourself."

"You telling me no?" she asked with a little tear in her voice.

"I'm telling you, Wanda, that you don't need to waste your money on me and Harold here."

"Speak for yourself," said Harold.

"I'm speaking the truth, Wanda," I said. "We gonna give you back your money because you wasted it with us."

"Speak for yourself," Harold repeated.

"Come on, Harold," I said. "We ain't gonna take no money that we don't deserve. You'll find someone who can do this job. Lots of men know how. We don't."

Funny end to this story was a few months later it was the week before Thanksgiving and the F&J was jammed. Between sets, I seen Wanda come in wearing this skin-tight red dress. She was looking fine. Came up to me and said, "Hey, baby, I'm cooking Thanksgiving dinner and wondering if you'd come by."

Being so far from my Louisiana home, I was much obliged.

"Sure thing," I said.

Thanksgiving was a lovely day. She cooked a turkey just like her mama from Mississippi had taught her. She made the biscuits from scratch. The greens and sweet potatoes had me thinking of my mama. Her kids were well behaved and sweet as they could be.

After dinner we talked about the kind of life she wanted to have once she put enough money away. She wanted to buy a house back down South. She wanted to make sure her kids graduated high school. She talked to me like I was family. I didn't make a move on her to have sex. I knew she'd had enough sex from enough men. She didn't invite me over for sex. She didn't want sex; she wanted a friend.

Wasn't that I didn't want sex. I did. But being careful kept me from chasing anything crazy—or at least that's what I thought. I'd been living in Chicago many months—maybe even a year—before I got me my first little piece. Happened at the Squeeze, the same club where the man walked in with his wife's head in a paper bag.

Cute little gal came over to me. I appreciated that because I was no good at making the first move.

"Been watching you for some time," she said.

"Thank you, ma'am."

"But I'm just wondering one thing. It's a personal thing. Mind if I ask?"

"Go ahead."

"I wanna know you if you make love as wild as you play that guitar."

Naturally, the question excited me. Right then and there my blood started to rise.

"All I can say is that I do my best," I said.

"Well, my style is wild."

"I like wild," I assured her.

"But I also get a little rough beforehand. You know what I mean?"

"Not exactly, but I'm willing to find out."

"If there's some fighting first, the fucking gets better."

No woman had ever come on to me and used the word "fucking" before. The word got me even more excited.

"In the name of love," I said, "I'll do a little fighting."

When we got up to her room, though, turned out she was all talk. She'd been drinking so long that she fell right to sleep. Being a gentleman, I didn't wanna wake her. Got in bed next to her and fell asleep myself. Was the middle of the night when I felt this *whack!* across my back. Damned if she wasn't whipping me with my own belt. She hit me so hard my back was bleeding.

"You ready to fight?" she asked, all smiles.

I was hurting, and I wasn't about to take this shit lying down. I went for her, and she was happy.

"Now," she said, "you'll see what real fucking is all about."

She wasn't wrong.

Chess Moves

The gunslingers had different styles. Some of the cats—like Magic Sam and Otis Rush—were quick at the draw and didn't mind showing you how they did it. Like the Mud, they were teachers who felt that the lessons should be passed on. Other cats didn't look at it that way.

Earl Hooker wasn't interested in teaching you nothing. He was too busy looking over his shoulder.

When I first got attention on the bandstand, I noticed Earl Hooker listening hard to my licks. Believe me when I tell you I wasn't playing half of what he could play, but I could see him studying my guitar and amp.

Couple nights later I come to discover my amp is sounding different. I'm also missing my long wire that lets me wander all around when I play. Someone said they saw Earl messing with my equipment during one the breaks. So on a Saturday I decided to go over to where he stayed with his mama and pay the man a visit.

His mother told me, "He's asleep."

Well, this was four in the afternoon. Of course musicians tend to work all night and sleep all day, so I understood. His mama went about her business, and I was set to leave when I heard a loud snore coming from the bedroom where the door was ajar. I tiptoed over, stuck my head in, and sure enough, there was my guitar wire and a couple of tubes that I recognized as belonging to my amp.

"Hooker," I said. "Wake up, man. What you doing with my wire and my tubes?"

He came to life, yawning and rubbing his eyes. "Just borrowing 'em, man. That's all."

"Don't you need to ask before you borrow?"

"I was curious to hear that sound you make. Wanted to see if it was the tubes."

"I want my wire back."

"Take it."

"And my tubes."

"I think they work better in my amp than yours," said Earl.

"I think they work right well in mine."

I took my stuff and left.

Even though I was pissed on that particular day, I couldn't harbor no bad feelings for Earl—he was too great for me to stay mad. Earl was the first one to get the hang of the wah-wah pedal. He was one of the first to use a double-neck guitar. He liked to experiment. He also liked telling stories. A couple of his stories killed me.

One had him and his band traveling way down into the Delta for a gig at a roadhouse. Owner said only way to attract a crowd was to go into the fields and tell the folk picking cotton when and where he'd be playing. Earl and his cats were wearing their old tuxes with the cummerbunds—the only clothes they brought—and they didn't wanna dirty 'em up.

"If you wanna get paid," the owner said, "then get out in them fields and advertise your show. Else you'll be playing to an empty house."

So Earl and his guys parked alongside a big cotton field where everyone was doing the afternoon picking.

"Playing down the road tonight," he told all the workers he met. "Gonna be playing the kinda music you like. My songs go good with drinking and dancing. It heats up the ladies real good."

After a while, here comes a white supervisor on a horse. The man was holding a rifle.

"What are you niggers doing out here in tuxedos?" he asked.

"We musicians," said Earl.

"Right out here you ain't. Out here you picking cotton."

"I don't think so," said Earl.

"Well, I do," said the man with the rifle.

For the next hour Earl Hooker and his band became the best-dressed cotton pickers in Mississippi.

That night at the roadhouse the crowd was small—and so was Earl's pay. On the ride back to Chicago stomachs were empty and funds were tight. So when the band stopped at a grocery by the side of the road, Earl had a plan: he'd go in and buy some soda pop and crackers. Meanwhile, his piano man, wearing a big overcoat—a mighty strange-looking outfit during the summertime—walked down the aisle where they had the canned meats.

"When the man isn't looking," Earl told his piano player, "slip some of that Vienna sausage in the pockets of your coat. Get all you can."

The plan worked. Earl bought the pop and crackers while his man got a whole mess of canned meats. They went down the road twenty or thirty miles before stopping in a little wooded area. They got out and spread back the grass so they could lay out the food and start to eat. Everyone got a soda pop and a few crackers. When it was time to break out the canned meat, the piano man emptied his pocket.

He had done stolen cans of Alpo dog food.

"What the fuck!" Earl cried. "Can't you read?"

"You know I can't," said the piano man.

"I forgot," Earl admitted, "but at least you could have picked the food that looked good."

"I did. Pictures on these cans make the food look real good."

When Earl told me this story I cracked up.

"What'd you do?" I asked him.

"You ever smelt a can of Alpo?" he asked.

"Sure," I said. "I got dogs."

"Well, that day Alpo didn't smell so bad. I went behind a tree, spread it over some crackers, and I ate the shit—that's what I did."

I related to Earl because, like me, he didn't read music. That came home to me some years later when word went out that Bobby Blue Bland was looking for a guitarist to replace Pat Hair. By then Bobby was a big earner. He worked all the time, and guitarists saw this as a great steady gig.

Pat, by the way, got dealt a bad hand. One night after playing with Bobby, he went back to the motel. He was up in bed when he heard some people at his door. When they broke the door down, he grabbed his pistol and started shooting, but it was the cops who broke down the door. They'd come to the wrong room, but that didn't matter 'cause was one of the cops was dead and Pat was off to jail in Minneapolis. Just to pay my respects to a great guitarist, I went to that prison to visit him.

His absence left a big gap, and Bobby Blue Bland came to Chicago to audition cats to replace him. I didn't show up because I knew I couldn't cut it. In the Chicago blues world, everyone looked at Muddy as the biggest star—he had the most charisma of anyone—but Earl Hooker was the best guitarist. Earl was tired of hustling from gig to gig and was the first to come to the audition. When Bobby showed him the lead sheets, though, Earl didn't know what to make of them. (Neither, by the way, did Bobby Blue Bland, who also didn't read.) It came down to two cats that had no problems with notes on the page—Matt Murphy and Wayne Bennett. Wayne was the slicker of the two and got the gig. He and Bobby lived happily ever after.

When Willie Dixon said he wanted me to come down to Chess for a session, the first thing I worried about was notes on the page. Only other time I was at Chess was when Wayne Bennett borrowed my Gibson. I watched Wayne read the charts with no problem. I figured session players had to read.

"Can't read no notes on the page," I told Willie.

"Don't matter. You can feel what to do."

This was after Eli Toscano had been fished out of Lake Michigan and Dixon was back at Chess.

"Who'll I be playing for?"

"The Wolf."

"The Wolf got Hubert Sumlin. He don't need me."

"Him and Hubert got into a fistfight. Hubert say he's through."

"If I don't play the right notes, I don't want the Wolf beating on me."

"He won't. You'll be in and out in an hour. An easy ten bucks."

I agreed.

When I get to the studio at 2120 South Michigan, first thing I heard was, "Motherfucker, you standing in the wrong place."

That was the Wolf talking. I didn't do nothing, though, 'cause I didn't know who he was talking to.

"Motherfucker," he repeated, "did you hear what I said?"

"You mean me?" I asked.

"Yes, motherfucker. Who else would I mean?"

"Well, my name's Buddy, not motherfucker."

"Up in here," said the Wolf, "everyone's a motherfucker. Now get closer to the mic."

Can't remember what song we played that day, but I do remember not saying one single word during the session. I also remember Leonard Chess coming out the recording booth, changing the tempo, and giving Wolf some ideas. I figured Chess was a guy who just turned on the lights and let the musicians do their thing, but I was wrong. Chess had lots of different notions about how the music should go. I saw that Wolf didn't mind listening to him.

From that day forward I stuck to my policy for playing a Chess session. Don't talk. Lay low. Listen. Figure out what the star was doing. Figure out what the star needed. Support the star. Help the star sound better. Don't worry about bringing no attention to me because the session ain't about me. Stay the hell outta the spotlight.

My policy paid off. Because I learned in a hurry to be a good team player, I got more calls. Muddy called me to record with him. Sonny Boy Williamson and Jimmy Rogers and Little Walter called me to record with them. I got a reputation as someone who could make it to a session on time and fill in whatever little gaps needed filling.

First thing I noticed when I played those sessions was Willie Dixon putting his name on the songs. I started to realize that being a writer meant you got more money. Second thing I saw was a bottle of whiskey on top of the piano. Leonard Chess never failed put it there. I asked Willie why.

"Leonard ain't dumb," said Willie. "He knows what sells records is capturing the same feeling we capture in the club.

There's booze in the club and he wants booze on the record. He don't want us drunk, but he wants us lit. He wants to feel the fire that the folks get to feeling in the club."

Still not much of drinker, I didn't indulge. I was too scared of tripping up the star with a wrong note. I needed all my concentration to stay out the way. In doing that, I saw that I was creating two Buddy Guys.

The first was the wild guy in the club with the long cord and the crazy style, the guy who never sat down and didn't care if the amp was too loud and distorted with fuzz tones. That Buddy Guy liked the fuzz tones 'cause they added to the wildness. Wilder I got, happier the customers.

The second Buddy Guy was the mild-mannered studio cat. Just tell me where to sit and I'll do the rest—quietly. I'll provide whatever little touches you need. I'll take whatever little cash you paying. It's enough for me to play with the Mud and the Wolf. It ain't about the money—it's about soaking up wisdom.

In the club you got time to heat up the crowd. On a record, you got to come with it right away. The greats knew how to do that. They screamin' out the gate. They telling you, "You gonna buy this record cause I'll fuckin' make you."

At the same time, being with the greats also broke my heart. It broke that dream I had back in Baton Rouge that the greats were living in mansions and driving gold Cadillacs. Of all the greats, only Muddy had a house. His was at 4339 South Lake Park, a place I'd get to know real well. The others, living in little rooms, could barely scratch up a living. Don't know how many records Chess was selling and don't know the breakdown of the bookkeeping. I do know, though, that Chess wasn't big in sharing the profits.

Along those lines, I learned a lot the day that Willie told me Lightnin' Hopkins was coming over to his house. I ran there to meet him. I felt like one of the disciples running to meet Jesus.

Jesus might have drunk wine, but not like Lightnin'. It was early afternoon and he was already preaching strong. He was a thin man with a gravel voice, dark glasses, big black hat, and much shit to say. As an agent for Leonard Chess, Willie was trying to talk him into a record deal involving future royalties.

"Fuck future royalties," said Lightnin'. "Fuck Leonard Chess and fuck you, Willie Dixon. Royalties don't mean shit to me."

"Royalties bought Muddy Waters a house right here in Chicago," said Willie.

"Muddy does it his way," said Lightnin'. "I do it mine. Mine is simple. Pay me a hundred dollars and I'll record a song. Don't wanna see no contract, don't wanna hear about no legal nothing. You give me a hundred, I give you a song."

"That's the old way of doing it, Lightnin'," said Willie. "That way you wind up cheating yourself."

"Maybe, but my way I wind up with a hundred dollars. Your way, I wind up with nothing."

"But the contract is binding."

"I don't know how to read no contract."

"A lawyer can help you."

"A lawyer will take my money. Feel the same about the lawyer as I do Leonard Chess. Lawyer wants me to sing a song, he gotta give me a hundred dollars."

Willie shook his head.

"Shake your fuckin' head all you want, Willie Dixon, but I been out here for a minute now. I seen what there is to see. Record companies always got ways to prove there ain't no profits. And if there ain't no profits, they say there ain't no royalties. Up-front only money you ever gonna get."

Willie kept arguing, but Lightnin' didn't budge. I knew Lightnin', with his country Texas wisdom, was right. Problem was, though, I couldn't even command a hundred dollars to record a song. I was lucky to get ten dollars to *play* on a song. I'd have to go through a lot of changes before I could put Lightnin's lessons to good use.

The first little sign of any change happened at the end of the fifties, when I'd look up from my gig at 708 or Theresa's or the Squeeze and see a few white faces in the crowd. My first thought was that they had to be cops. In those days whites didn't come around the South Side or the West Side to hear no blues. If they was cops, that meant we couldn't go outside during the break with open bottles 'cause that was against the law. We could bribe the cops, but who wanted to waste money like that? Seeing cops just made us nervous.

Come to find out, though, they wasn't cops. They was young fans. One guy called himself Paul Butterfield and said he played harp. Another was Michael Bloomfield. He said he played guitar. They didn't come up to play at first—they were too scared—but after a while they built up their nerves and they joined in on a jam. I was surprised and happy to hear that the blues wasn't no hobby for them. They'd been listening hard, and they were learning to play hard. That's one of the first times I realized that the blues was blue, not white or black.

I could hear how Butterfield had studying the harp players around town. I'd been doing the same. It wasn't my instrument, but more than my instrument, the harp made the sound of a man moaning. That's a sound I love.

Little Walter turned his harmonica upside down and played it bottoms up. He sucked so much sound outta that thing you'd think it was two men playing it. Walter was small, but like Wolf, he was a fighter. And he wasn't shy about talking up his talent. He was famous for saying, "I get more outta my harmonica than George Washington Carver got out of a peanut."

One night up at Theresa's I saw there was a whole gang of those harmonica cats hanging around. Thought I'd have me some fun.

Went up to Junior Wells, another wild man, who had taken Little Walter's place in Muddy's band. Said to Junior, "Walter's here, and he says you shouldn't even be sitting in the same club as him."

Said to Shakey Horton, "James Cotton is here and he says there's room for only one real harp man in this here bar."

Told Sonny Boy Williamson, "All these others think they can blow you off the stage."

And finally I leaned over to Walter and whispered, "These cats are gunning for you. What you gonna do?"

Well, they all got up and came to the stage, looking to wear the crown. I had my band play "Juke." Of course that gave Walter the advantage 'cause "Juke" was his hit, but the others knew the song good as Walter. Problem is that they couldn't play it as good. They couldn't play any song good as Walter.

That didn't keep 'em from trying, and an hour later, by the end of that set, I do believe I heard the best harmonica playing anyone's every heard anywhere. I'd give a million dollars for a tape of that night.

The friendly competition didn't end there. That night the boys recognized that Little Walter couldn't be topped. Even Junior

Wells—my future partner and a very proud man—had to admit Little Walter had pissed on everyone.

Talkin' 'bout pissing, there was so much drinking after that jam that the boys kept running back and forth from the bathroom. At one point Junior and Walter had gone to the men's room at the same time.

"I saw you in there, motherfucker," said Walter. "Heard you been telling the ladies you got a log in your pants. All I saw was a stick."

"A stick," Junior shot back, "a lot longer than yours."

"None of y'all can even stand at the same piss stand as me," said James Cotton.

"Motherfuckers," said Sonny Boy, "if you want to talk about God-given equipment, I'm ready to measure my manhood against anyone."

Right then and there, out came the dicks! And out came the women—running over to see these fools looking to claim bragging rights for carrying the biggest tool in the shed.

I'd seen Muddy play a similar game. Most nights he liked to sit and play, but there were times when he was feeling good so he stood up to sing. If he was feeling really good, he'd dance. And if he felt extra-special good, before he got up there, he'd take a bottle of beer, shake it up, and slip it in his trousers. When he'd get to singing that line that said, "Ain't that a man!" he'd unzip his trousers, grab the bottle of beer sticking up like a hard-on, unpop the top, and watch the foam spray all over the ladies dancing in front of him. Man, them women went wild!

Wildness in women wasn't my speed. I could see it was an exciting thing for most men. And I ain't saying there weren't times when a lady took me to the dark end of the street for a good ol' wild time. But as a steady diet, I couldn't handle it real well.

Every man has his own thing with women. Muddy, for instance, loved the young girls. He had this song that said, "She's nineteen years old and got ways like a baby child." He sang that he couldn't please her, but that was just the song. In real life Muddy found many a nineteen-year-old he could please. He also was a jealous man. He had a habit of beating up on his women. Of course at that time many men did the same. And many women urged them on—like the way the woman with the belt urged me. It was a different era. Billie Holiday used to sing, "If I get beat up by my poppa, ain't gonna call no copper," almost like getting beat up was like getting loved.

I don't like being violent with women. Fact is that I don't like being violent period. But in the world of Chicago, where farm boys like Muddy had come to the big city and electrified their blues, violence was everywhere. If Muddy came in the club and said, "Man, I'm dead tired. I think my old lady's sneaking on me and I had to take a strap to her," none of us said nothing. Because Muddy had lots of old ladies and because he believed in keeping them in line, we heard this kind of talk all the time. That was his way.

It was also his way to be extra sweet to young women who he wasn't hitting on—and protect them when they needed protection. Even today you'll meet females who will tell you that Muddy was the best friend they ever had. They'll say how he took the time to teach them to stay out of trouble. They loved to call him Daddy. When it came to the ladies, there were a lot of sides to Muddy.

By December of 1959 I'd been in Chicago two years and two months. I was twenty-three, and I'd done okay. I was making enough money with my guitar to have my own place. I bought a little used car that let me drive to Gary for the gig at F&J. I built up a name as a wild man in the clubs and a quiet man in the studio. I made two records with Cobra, and even though Cobra had sunk into Lake Michigan along with Eli Toscano, Willie Dixon and Leonard Chess was using me as a sideman. When I went to record, I was ready to put a pint in my pocket like the other cats. Women were noticing me like they notice most musicians. Women were calling on me, letting me know they was willing. That was nice, but it really wasn't what I wanted. I wanted something stable. I grew up in a stable house with a loving family. Family meant a lot to me, and if I could find the right woman and start a family of my own, maybe I could enjoy the same kind of happiness I'd seen Daddy enjoy with Mama.

I wanted kids. I wanted a wife. I wanted to stay in Chicago and see if could get more people to come out to hear my music. I wanted to make more records, and I figured that if I played my cards right, maybe Leonard Chess would put something out on me.

First, though, I wanted to take care of this loneliness. I wanted to get married.

"She's Nineteen"

I told you about Muddy's song where he sings about the nineteen-year-old honey. When I heard Muddy playing that, he was forty-seven. When I married Joan, I was twenty-three and she was nineteen. I'd actually met her a couple of years earlier when I first started living with Shorty. She was living in the same building with her mom, dad, and sisters. She was a pretty girl with a sweet personality who gave me the love I was looking for.

I remember coming home from an out-of-town gig with Jimmy Rogers, the great guitarist with Little Walter in Muddy's original band that played Jewtown before the band made records. We pulled up to Jimmy's house where his wife was waiting. When he got out the car, my drummer, Fred Below, said to his wife, "Don't worry, he didn't do nothing bad. He was a good boy."

"I ain't worried," said Mrs. Rogers. "Don't nobody want him but me."

I liked the way that sounded. I wanted to be a man married to a woman who wouldn't worry when I was gone and could say, "Don't nobody want him but me." That felt comfortable to me.

I thought I had that woman in Joan. We was happy, but her daddy wasn't. He didn't like me. He didn't see me being very successful.

"You working?" he asked when I told him I wanted to marry his daughter.

"Work all the time, sir."

"Where?"

I told him.

"Those are barrooms. You tending bar?"

"No, sir," I said. "I think you know I'm a musician."

"I been in those barrooms, son, and I see that the bartenders get better tips than the musicians."

"That might be true."

"So why ain't you tending bar?"

"'Cause I like playing my guitar."

"You might like it, but from what I hear, the people don't like you near as well as Muddy Waters. Muddy Waters got him his own house. You got a house of your own?"

"No, sir, but one day I hope to."

"When's that day coming, son?"

"Can't say for sure."

"Can't say for sure. Well, what can you say? Can you say when you gonna be making real money?"

"I'm doing okay. Playing in Gary."

"You playing everywhere, boy, but I don't see no new car and I don't see no down payment for a house. If you going to Gary, get a job at the steel mill. Steel mill pays. At the steel mill you don't gotta worry 'bout no tips. Steady salary is something you can count on. That there guitar of yours is like a child's toy. You gotta get you a man's job."

I wasn't about to argue with my future father-in-law. Out of respect to Joan I wanted to show respect. But I didn't like the man any more than he liked me. He complained about all the barrooms where I worked, but he was a big drinker himself. I could try to defend myself. I could tell him that Muddy Waters himself said I was good. So did Magic Sam and Otis Rush. The Wolf wanted to take me on the road—and the Wolf didn't ask just anybody. I could tell him that I was respected. Club owners liked me because I showed up on time and entertained the people real good. They called me dependable. When Chess was making a record, whether for Sonny Boy, Wolf, Walter, or the Mud, I was getting calls 'cause I could cut it. Problem, of course, was that none of this paid big money. And far as my future father-in-law was concerned, nothing mattered except money.

"Look," I told the man. "I hear you. I understand a man's gotta take care of his woman. And that's what I intend to do."

"I'm holding you to it," he said, before walking out of the room and heading to the corner bar.

Money was on my mind—it had to be. Marrying Joan at the end of 1959, I had to feed two. When our first child, Charlotte Renee, was born in 1961, I had to feed three.

"In this business," the Mud liked to say, "someone is always gonna come along and make more than you. When I started up in here, I was the big money-maker. Didn't see all that much for myself, but I got enough of a taste to where I was living good. Then here comes Chuck Berry up from St. Louis. When Leonard first heard Chuck, he threw him out. He didn't even understand. Chuck had to sell some blood to keep eating. But Chuck came back and Leonard changed his mind. Next thing you know, that 'Rock and Roll Music' was sweeping the country. Same thing with Bo Diddley. He had him this thing that got the kids to dancing. Leonard made big money off Bo. Now he got this big girl named Etta James. He got her going good with a song they're playing on the radio. Something about crying. Leonard's promoting the hell out of this girl. Now I'm not saying Leonard don't like the blues—he does—but Leonard likes money more. If he could make money selling polkas, we'd be recording polkas."

"But we doing the same thing, Mud," I said. "When I work a club, I got to look at the jukebox and make sure I can play those songs. I got to learn 'What I Say' and sing it like Ray Charles."

"That ain't gonna happen," said Muddy.

"Sure ain't, but I gotta try. Talkin' 'bout money, they've been playing a song called 'Money, That's What I Want.'"

"That song sounds like 'What'd I Say,'" said Muddy. "All them songs sound the same."

"That's what they say about the blues."

"The blues sound the same, but the singers are different one from the other."

"I like that 'Money.' I learned it. Been doing it almost every night. Gets everyone to dancing. I don't see nothing wrong with that."

"Look, son, you can't get me talking against no hit records. Everyone wants a hit. When I put out 'Mannish Boy' and 'Still a Fool' and 'Just Make Love to Me,' I wasn't complaining. Ain't complaining now. Just saying that these blues that you and I took from the plantation . . . man, I just don't want them blues to die."

"Me neither, Muddy."

"It's just something we gotta remember. The world might wanna forget about 'em, but we can't. We owe 'em our lives. Wasn't for them, we still be smelling mule shit."

First Time I Met the Blues

Gotta say that the first time Willie Dixon told me he was cutting a record on me, it took me by surprise.

"Wasn't easy," he said. "Leonard ain't that impressed by you as a solo man. He sees you strictly as backup. He thinks you good as backup, but that's as far as it goes. I told him differently. I said, 'I seen Buddy Guy tear the roof off Theresa's. That ain't no goddamn backup.'"

"I know I can the tear the roof off a record," I said.

"That's just the point—you can't. Leonard likes his records a certain way. You can't get all wild like you do on stage. Can't play too crazy. Can't fuck up the sound none like I seen you do in the clubs. Leonard likes his blues clean."

"You got the songs you want me to do?"

"I got all the songs you need."

"I got some songs I wrote myself."

"Well, we'll do mine first. Then we'll worry about yours."

The first one I cut wasn't written by either of us. It was a thing by Little Brother Montgomery called "First Time I Met the Blues."

When it came out, some people said I sounded like B. B. King, and I took that as a compliment. Who didn't wanna sound like B. B.? I liked the opening line that Little Brother wrote: "The first time I met the blues, I was walking down through the woods." I liked closing my eyes and pretending I was back home in them woods. Also liked that I had Otis Spann, the Mud's man, on piano, and Fred Below on drums. That same day I sang a song Willie put his name on—"Broken-Hearted Blues"—but everyone seemed to like "First Time" better.

Day after the session Willie told me that Leonard was putting out "First Time," but on one condition.

"What's that?" I asked.

"He wants you to change your name."

"Why don't he like my name?"

"Ain't that he don't like it," said Willie. "It's just he thinks you should be a King."

"What does that mean?"

"You know, you call yourself Buddy King or King Guy—something like that."

"Don't see the point. People might get me confused with B. B. or Freddie King."

"That's just the confusion Leonard wants. Only he calls it association. 'King' is associated with strong-selling blues."

"Muddy don't got no king in his name."

"He came through before the kings."

"Well, I'm coming through after."

"Buddy King sounds real good."

"Maybe, but it ain't me. Besides, when they play the record in Baton Rouge and the deejay calls out, 'Buddy King,' my people won't know it's me."

"You can tell your people ahead of time."

"That's ain't good enough. I want my mama and daddy to hear the name they gave me over the radio."

"Leonard won't be happy."

"I won't be happy if I don't go by my right name."

"You're gonna hold stubborn?"

"If you mean, am I gonna hold on to my name, yes, sir, I am."

I did, and I guess Leonard Chess thought "First Time I Met the Blues" was good enough to put out under Buddy Guy. When I went home to Louisiana for Christmas, I learned that they did play it on WXOK, causing my family and friends happiness and pride.

In the first few years of the sixties every now and then Chess recorded me. Sometimes Willie let me keep my name on songs I had written, but I was never told nothing about the publishing rights of the composer. I didn't know those rights belonged to me, and I didn't know that if they were transferred to someone else—like the Chess Brothers's publishing company—I should have been paid. Payment wasn't on my mind—I just wanted to make it.

Chess thought that if I was going to make it, I'd have to make it in the mold of a B. B. or a Freddie. They tried some instrumentals out on me, and they even tried some ballads, but nothing caught on. If I started in on what had become my live style—twisting the notes real hard, playing riffs that sounded like they came from outer space, letting the tape buzz and bleed with different combinations that caught your ear—Leonard would say, "Buddy, you're doing too much. Play less. Calm your ass down."

I'd be a fool to argue, so I didn't. Leonard was holding all the cards, and I was at the bottom of the Chess totem pole. At the same time, I was still a young man in my mid-twenties. Having my own records out there impressed everyone . . . except my father-in-law. When me and my wife showed him that 45 of "First Time I Met the Blues," he said, "They give you this record instead of money?"

"What do you mean?" I asked.

"I mean, did they hand you cash for playing this here record?"

"No, but I signed a contract that says if it sells a certain amount, I get paid royalties."

He laughed in my face. "Son," he said, "when those royalties come in, dogs gonna be fucking pigs."

The man was right. He was saying the same thing Lightnin' Hopkins had said. Deep down, I agreed, but was too proud to admit it.

Wasn't too proud, though, to double-up my work. I needed money and wasn't afraid to go after it.

When Elmore James, for example, told me I could make good money playing this gig with him down in Texas, I figured it was far away but worth it. We piled into Elmore's station wagon and drove to a roadhouse just below the Arkansas-Texas border. Place was packed. We played three long sets and were ready for the long ride back. Time to get paid.

Big bear of a man came to the bandstand while we was putting away our instruments. He was the guy who called Elmore for the gig.

"Bad news," said the bear.

"What bad news?" asked Elmore.

"We done got robbed."

"I didn't see no robbery."

"Happened out back. We clean out of money."

"That won't do," said Elmore.

"Gonna have to do," said the bear.

"Oh, man, this is some fucked-up shit," said Elmore. "Least you can do is give us gas money to get back to Chicago."

Bear refused.

Elmore started screaming at him, which is when the bear put a gun to his head. That got us to leave without no more arguing.

We had enough gas to get to East St. Louis, where we had to beg strangers to give us $5, which took us to the Chicago city limits. From there I reached in my pocket and used my last fifteen cents for bus fare home.

This made me reevaluate my situation: loved music more than anything. Would rather play music than anything. But playing music wasn't paying my bills. So when I had a chance at a steady job, I took it. It happened when a man in Joliet asked me to manage his club. He saw that not only could I play, but I could also organize. I could get names like Wolf, Walter, and Muddy down there. Joliet's only forty-five minutes from Chicago, and using my rhythm section like I had in Gary, I could convince big-name bluesmen to come in, do a few songs, and make it back to their regular gigs in time for their late sets. To kick things off, though, I thought it best to get one of the stars to play from ten to two. Because I wanted the music fans in Joliet to know I wasn't fooling around, I booked Sonny Boy Williamson. (This is Sonny Boy 2; I never knew the original Sonny Boy.)

Club 99 was a good-sized room. Owner gave me a little room in the back so, after playing Friday night till 4 or 5 a.m., I could sleep and be right there to get ready for Saturday.

On this particular Saturday morning the owner came to my room to say that Sonny Boy had arrived for that night's gig and was at the bar drinking.

"What time is it?" I asked.

"Not yet noon. You better go out there and see about him."

I went out and saw Sonny Boy sitting in front of a fifth of whiskey.

"Morning," I said.

"Morning, motherfucker."

"You here bright and early."

"Damn right," he said. "Had nothing to do today, so I figure this is good a place as any to pass the time."

Owner whispered in my ear, "He ain't gonna be fit to play tonight. Say something."

Knowing Sonny Boy, I decided saying something wouldn't be wise.

Later that same afternoon I was napping when the owner came back knocking at my door.

"Your friend's still at the bar," he said, "still drinking."

Just then I heard the sound of his harp. Went out to the club, and there was Sonny Boy, playing his harmonica to the woman cleaning up the bar. When he blew harp, he could do it without hands. He'd curl his upper lip to hold the harmonica and blow it with his nose. You wouldn't think that could sound good, but Sonny Boy made it sound great. The gal had a smile across her face, and Sonny Boy had another big fifth set in front of him.

"Say something," said the owner.

Hadn't changed my mind. I knew these guys. They weren't the kind who could be told when and when not to drink. I left him alone, but I admit I was worried. In just a few hours I'd be calling him to the stage. I was afraid that he'd never make it—or, like Jimmy Reed, he'd fall on his face. If that happened, the crowd would start booing and I'd probably lose this job.

Come 9:30, it was time to hit. Sonny Boy was nowhere in sight. The owner gave me a look like I had murdered his mother.

"Where the fuck is that harmonica player? I told you he was going drink himself into the gutter. What you gonna do now?"

"We'll heat up the crowd with a few warm-up numbers," I said.

Up on stage, I kept looking around for Sonny Boy. The man was still missing.

Finally, after playing a third song, I knew it was star time. Everyone had come to hear Sonny Boy Williamson. I figured I might as well give it a shot. What else could I do?

"Ladies and gentleman," I announced. "Let's give a warm welcome to the great Sonny Boy Williamson!"

Ten seconds passed. The owner looked at me and I looked back at him. He shrugged, and then I shrugged, and then out of nowhere Sonny Boy Williamson jumped on that stage with the energy of a teenager. At that time he had to be seventy, but you'd never know it by how he moved. He started in with "Don't Start Me to Talkin'," went into "Keep It to Yourself" and "Fattening Frogs for Snakes," and then burned down the house with the song that says, "Stop your off-the-wall jive . . . if you don't treat me no better, it's gonna be your funeral and my trial."

Long story short, Sonny Boy played for two straight hours. Around midnight he took a break, but the break only lasted long enough for him to have a couple more drinks. Then he was back up, rocking the joint till 2 a.m. We couldn't get him off the stage. When he did get off, he made a beeline for the bar and started to drink. Me and the owner were there to thank him for a job well done.

"Fuck both of y'all," he said. "I heard you talkin' bad 'bout me this morning. You was saying I was gonna be too drunk to play. Well, lemme tell you something. When I was twenty-nine, doctor says, 'Sonny Boy, if you don't put down the bottle you'll never see thirty-five.' Guess where that doctor is now?"

"Where?" I had to know.

"Pushin' up motherfuckin' daisies."

We had to laugh.

"So let's drink to his health," said Sonny Boy, as we all raised our glasses. "Fuck y'all and fuck the dead doctor."

Even though I was managing Club 99 in Joliet to make ends meet, I was still gigging in Chicago. I used to play Curly's at Madison and Holman. I liked Curly and got sad when he said that business was so bad he might have to close up. It was more than me worrying about losing a gig—I hated it when any blues club had to shut down. I took it personally.

"If I brought B. B. King up in here," I asked Curly, "would that help business?"

"Sure as shit would."

B. B. was playing Gary. I drove up and told him the situation. "Curly's a good guy," I said, "but these other clubs around here are running him out of business. I'd like to help the brother."

B. B. responded with two words: "Me too."

So I ran back to Chicago and told Curly B. B. would come in that weekend.

"That ain't ever gonna happen," he said. "B. B King ain't showing up. He don't give a fuck about saving no blues joint."

That Saturday night I got to Curly's around 1 a.m. Club was jammed, but B. B. wasn't there.

Curly was fit to be tied. Steam was coming off the top of his head. "You and your B. B. King are both no-good, lowdown dogs. I told you he'd never show."

"But . . ."

"I don't hear no buts. I don't need no lame excuses. Told all these folks they'd get to hear B. B. King, and they looked at me like I was crazy. Well, I was."

"No you wasn't," I said. "He just went to park his car."

Right then B. B. came walking down the street. You better believe he was carrying Lucille. When he walked into Curly's, it was like Santa Claus coming down the chimney. Everyone was up and screaming. That night he played for free. Curly's got a good name and folks started flocking in.

Thing about B. B.—then and now—is his humility. Mama used to talk about a humble heart being a good heart. But in my lifetime I've met few genuinely humble people, especially in the music business, where most everyone gets what John Lee Hooker calls the Big Head. B. B. never had no big head. Even today every conversation with him almost gets me to crying because I feel how sincere he is about his love of people and music.

At Curly's that night, after he got through playing, he wanted to know where we could go to hear good jazz. I knew all the jazz joints because, like B. B., I couldn't hear enough good jazz. We went down to the Trocadero to catch Gene Ammons—they called him Jug because of how he liked to drink—and sat there till the sun came up, listening to this man crying through his tenor saxophone.

"You know," I said, "I love this jazz, but sometimes I don't think the jazz cats love me."

"Some of 'em can get a little attitude," B. B. agreed.

"The other day I was standing outside Pepper's with Jerry, my horn player, when a jazz cat comes up to him and says, 'Hey, man, who you giggin' with?'

"Jerry says, 'Buddy Guy.'

"Cat doesn't know me. He figures I'm another sideman. He turns to Jerry and says, 'Buddy Guy? The wild man who comes in off the street with that long cord?'

"'Yeah,' says Jerry.

"Cat says, 'How can you play that shit? How can you play such simple-minded crap?'

"'I like it,' says Jerry.

"'Well, to each his own. By the way, man, can I borrow a couple of bucks?'

"'No,' says Jerry.

"'Well, at least give me a taste of that wine you drinking.'

"'No.'

"'How 'bout a hit off that reefer you smoking?'

"'No.'

"'Damn, motherfucker, why you gotta be so cold?'

"'Cause I paid for this wine and reefer by playing the music you calling shit. I don't wanna contaminate you none. But I do wanna introduce you to Buddy Guy. He standing right here.'

"Cat nearly falls out. I just smile and offer my hand. 'Pleasure to meet you,' is all I say."

B. B. laughed and said, "Buddy, I got a story for you. Ran into Miles Davis up in New York. Never met the man before, but he comes up to me and says, 'You bad, man. You real bad.' I say, 'Thank you, Miles.' He say, 'Not only are you bad, you can do something I can't.' 'What's that, Miles?' 'I been studying music my whole life,' says Miles. 'Went to school. Had all these fancy teachers and fancy courses. But you, you bend one note and make more money in one night than I make in a month.'"

As a money-maker, B. B was always king, but the rest of us, even though we might work regular, struggled hard. That's why I kept

My loving family. From the left, my brother, Phil Guy, sister, Fannie Mae Guy, brother, Sam Guy, sister, Annie Mae Holmes, and I. *Courtesy of Victoria Fadden*

Teachers King, Hooker, Dixon.
Courtesy of Paul Natkin

John Lee, the freest of all the blues poets.
Courtesy of Paul Natkin

With Junior, brother for life. *Courtesy of Paul Natkin*

My jheri curl days.
Courtesy of Paul Natkin

Eric Clapton, forever friend.
Courtesy of Paul Natkin

Keith Richards, loyal and true.
Courtesy of Paul Natkin

A man who made a difference: Clifford Antone. *Courtesy of Victoria Fadden*

Jeff Beck and Ron Wood, fellow travelers. *Courtesy of Paul Natkin*

Generations converge, Jonny Lang and Ron Wood.
Courtesy of Paul Natkin

Robert Cray helped boost the blues.
Courtesy of Paul Natkin

My best friend B. B.
Courtesy of Paul Natkin

My latest and greatest club. Legends, 700 S. Wabash. *Courtesy of Paul Natkin*

In the basement in my jumpsuit phase.
Courtesy of Paul Natkin

Muddy, my main man.
Courtesy of Paul Natkin

My beloved father. *Courtesy of Paul Natkin*

my mouth shut and went along with whatever program I could fit into. If Leonard Chess wasn't interested in promoting my records, I wasn't about to complain. The man, after all, was giving me work in the studio. He saw me as a musical plumber. I could fix what needed fixing.

Six one morning the phone rang. It was Willie Dixon. "Leonard wants you to come down to the studio," he said.

"Tonight?"

"No, motherfucker, right now."

Didn't argue. Threw on my clothes and went to 2120. It was a session for the Wolf. You know they'd been drinking all night. But now it was morning, and the happy spirit of the whiskey had turned sour. Everyone looked like they lost their mama. Wolf looked like he was ready to whup everyone's ass. Leonard Chess looked like he hadn't slept in a week. He was yelling at Hubert Sumlin that Hubert wasn't getting this rhythm thing right. Hubert's a great guitarist, but there was bad communication 'tween him and Leonard.

I was sitting in the corner watching all this when Leonard turned and noticed me.

"How long you been sitting there?" he asked.

"A while," I said.

"Why didn't you say something?"

"'Cause no one asked me nothing."

I was one of these don't-speak-till-you're-spoken-to guys.

"Come over here, motherfucker," Leonard said. "Bring your guitar. Listen to what I'm humming to Hubert."

I listened.

"You hear it?" Leonard asked.

"I do."

"Can you play it?"

"I can."

And I did.

"Shit," said Leonard, "I've been looking to get this lick down for six hours. This guy comes waltzing in and nails it in a minute. Let's roll tape."

One take and we was done.

The Mighty Mojo

In the summer of 1960, when Muddy Waters tore up the Newport Jazz Festival singing "Got My Mojo Working," things slowly started to change for us blues guys. Muddy cracked open a door. It'd take a while for that door to open completely, but when it did, we started playing places we never dreamed of playing before. A few years later another door cracked open over in London. When that door opened completely, everything went topsy-turvy. What it came down to was white people paying money to hear the blues.

"Never seen nothing like it before," Muddy said a few days after he got back from Newport. I was over at his house, where we was watching a White Sox game on the television. Muddy loved the Sox. His hair was up in curlers and, as he liked to do, he was sitting around in his black silk drawers and undershirt. I think James Cotton was living somewhere in Muddy's house—he came in and out the room while we was talking—and even though Little Walter hadn't been in Muddy's band for years, he was staying there as well. The Mud's home life was always changing. He had different women stashed in different places. He had different musicians living with him at different times. But no matter what, he gave the orders. He was the daddy. And even though he wouldn't hesitate roughing up a woman, seems like the more he got known for that, the more women he got.

That day he was all excited about what happened at Newport. "I wasn't even sure about riding a thousand miles in the car, doing one night, and then riding back the next day. Especially this being called a jazz festival. Them jazz fans can be snobby. Jazz fans ain't known for loving no blues. I almost didn't go, but Buddy, I'd been a fool if I hadn't. Folk went crazy for us. I'm not talking about colored folk. I'm telling you I looked out there and seen nothing but white faces. Day before we got there, there was a riot. You know that?"

"Hadn't heard."

"Yes, sir," said Muddy. "They had Ray Charles—that was on a Saturday night—and folks went out their minds. Now I know Ray Charles had a band that can play some jazz, but it wasn't jazz that worked up the crowd. It was when he sang 'What'd I Say' and all that other stuff to get you to dancing. By the time we got up there—this was Sunday—they was warning us to play slow 'cause they don't want no more riots. You know me, Buddy, I don't mind sitting down when I play. But this crowd had me up and dancing until you'd think I was Elvis goddamn Presley. Should've been there, Buddy. Should've seen this shit for yourself."

"Wish I had."

"John Lee was there. He'll tell you. He said he ain't seen nothing like it neither."

Muddy was not a man given to exaggeration. Couple of years before he'd gone to England and come back downhearted. "They was looking for Big Bill Broonzy, not me," he'd told me when he got back. "They don't think a bluesman should have no electricity hooked up to his guitar. When they heard the sound coming out my amp, they started booing. Who told them that electricity fucks up the blues? All it do is make it louder. Ain't they ever heard of T-Bone Walker? He been electrical since way back been. You ain't gonna tell me T-Bone ain't blues. I think them English folk got their heads up their ass."

But then, right around Newport, something else started to happen. Folk music got hot. Kingston Trio records were selling like hotcakes. Lightnin' came through Chicago talkin' 'bout different colleges where he was playing. He described the audiences the way Muddy had described Newport. "Baby," Lightnin' told me, "I look out there into a sea of white cotton. Only it ain't cotton—it's college kids paying to hear the same shit I been playing down in Houston for years. Funny part is that they pay me more if I come up there without no pickup or amp. They want that old wooden guitar sound. They was calling that folk music."

John Lee was having the same good fortune. His attitude, though, always came back to money. When I got to know him some years later, he liked to say, in his stuttering way, "They c-c-c-c-c-can call it whatever the f-f-f-f-f-f-fuck they want. Long as they p-p-p-p-p-p-p-pay."

Seeing how white audiences were going for folk music and seeing how Muddy was starting to play folk festivals, Leonard Chess had the idea of turning Muddy into a folk artist. I heard about this from the Mud himself.

"'Cause all this folk music is selling hot and heavy, Leonard thinks I can get in on it," he said. "He told me last night he wants to get a record right away. Nothing electrical. Said he might not even turn on the lights. He wants it to sound like ol' time Delta. Says that's the original folk music. He wants two guitars—me and someone from back home who ain't been changed up by what they callin' Chicago blues. I told him to set up the studio tomorrow. I said I got my man."

"Who?" I asked.

"You," he said.

Sure, I was pleased, but I wondered how Leonard took it.

"Haven't told him yet. He'll know when you show up tomorrow."

When I showed up the next day, Leonard came out of the control booth and asked, "What are you doing here? I got a Muddy session."

"I'm here for that session," I explained.

"No one sent for you."

"Muddy did."

"I told Muddy I wanted one of those Delta guitarists. Some guy with white hair and a broken-down guitar. What do you know about country blues, Buddy?"

"That's all I do know," I said. "Was raised up on 'em."

When Muddy showed up, Leonard gave him hell for choosing me. They went back and forth, but Muddy stayed stubborn as a mule.

"You want the old music," Muddy told Chess. "Well, this young man can play that old music in his sleep. Pull him off this session and I'm going home to sleep."

Leonard let me stay. This happened in 1963 when Muddy was fifty and I was twenty-seven. Muddy not only let me weave my little solos in between his, but he also let me sing. When we recorded, I put my chair real close to his. I never stopped looking in his eyes. And I never stopped smiling. That's how happy I was. The songs were tunes Muddy had been doing for a while—"My Home Is in the Delta," "Long Distance," "Country Boy," "Feel Like Going Home." Willie Dixon plucked the upright bass and

Clif James beat the drums. Nothing fancy. In a couple of hours we was through.

"Damn," Leonard said to me, pleased with everything, "you *can* sound like an old fart, can't you?"

Muddy was happy too. All he wanted was someone who spoke his language and could follow his lead. They called the record *Muddy Waters: Folk Singer.*

About a month later the Mud went back to England, this time all prepared to be the folk singer. No electricity, no amp. He remembered how last time they didn't think he was authentic. Now he was ready to prove 'em wrong.

A week after he got back I stopped by the house to see him. It was five in the afternoon, but he wasn't up yet. If there was no White Sox on TV, Muddy liked to sleep the day away. I waited down in the kitchen, talking to Junior Wells, who was staying with him. Seemed like at some point everyone stayed with Muddy. I believe I was the exception. I liked being on my own. Besides, by then our second daughter, Carlise DeEtta, was born. I had a family to tend to.

Muddy came down around six. His hair was hidden under a black silk do-rag.

"How was England?" I asked.

"Shitty," he said. "They booed me again."

"How they be booing you when you gave 'em what they was looking for?" I asked.

"This time they was looking for the electricity. You see, when I was there last trip with the plugged-in guitar, a lot of the young kids liked it. So they went and got plugged-in guitars themselves. When I come back with the acoustic, they ain't happy. They don't want no quiet-ass folk singer. They want loud."

"Oh, man," I said, "That must have hurt."

"The money didn't hurt, but I'll be goddamned if I can figure out what those English motherfuckers want. Didn't I tell you they got their heads up their ass?"

My recording career still was going nowhere fast. I wrote a song called "Stone Crazy" that I thought might do something. Leonard put it out, along with some more I wrote—"I Found a True Love" "No Lie," "Watch Yourself." Someone said "Stone Crazy" popped on the Billboard chart for a minute, but I didn't see no check.

There was nothing wrong with any of these songs except for Chess telling me, "Keep your style under control." That meant, "Don't do your wild thing." My wild thing was when I let the guitar rip, when I didn't care if it was a little out of tune, didn't care if the feedback fucked up the sound. Fact is that I liked that fucked-up sound—it said what I needed to say.

No one loved the older cats more than I did. They were my heroes—Muddy and B. B. and Lightnin' hung the moon. And I could play in their style. I could play on the moon. But I could also go to Mars. Leonard Chess didn't want me up in Mars. Strangely, though, his son Marshall, who had fresher ears, was a space traveler like me. He kept telling his daddy to let me rock it my own way. Once they even had a big fight in the studio.

"You don't get what Buddy can really do," Marshall said to Leonard. "You've never seen him live in the club."

"I don't have to," Leonard shouted at his son. "I've seen what he can do in the studio. And what he does is fine."

"Then why do you keep in a straitjacket?"

"It's no straitjacket. It's a decision I make based on what radio wants to hear."

"You can't let radio lead you. You got to lead radio."

"I've done pretty good so far," said father to son. "Didn't I just get you a new car?"

"That's not the point, Dad. Music is changing, and Buddy's one of the artists pushing it in new directions."

"For now, let's stick to the directions leading to the bank."

Willie Dixon wrote a song with me in mind called "The Same Thing." He said it was a hit, the breakthrough I needed. He played it for me, and I liked it real well. It talked about men seeing women wearing their skirts tight being the same thing that makes a tomcat fight all night. It was a funky thing, and I was ready to run in and record it.

"No, sir," said Willie. "We gonna work this one right. We gonna rehearse it before we go in the studio. I ain't taking no chances."

That's what we did. For several months I was over at Willie's, running down this one song. We got it to the point where we was all convinced it was perfect.

I arrived early for the session. This was as good a chance as any for a surefire smash. What "Hideway" had done for Freddie King, "The Same Thing" could do for me.

Before we got started Leonard Chess came out the recording booth and asked me and Willie to run the song down. Leonard hadn't heard it before. I sang and played it, Leonard all the while nodding with the groove. He had a smile across face. That had to be a good sign.

It wasn't.

Leonard said, "Man, that's a goddamn hit song if I've ever heard one. Call Muddy."

"What do you want with Muddy?" asked Willie.

"I want Muddy to do it," said Leonard. "This tune's got Muddy written all over it. We'll find another song for Buddy."

I started to say something, started to protest how I'd been perfecting the song for months. But it wasn't my place to say anything—Willie had to speak up. But Willie didn't. Willie worked for Leonard, and Willie saw no reason to upset the boss.

Far as I was concerned, going against Muddy would be worse than going against my own mama—I loved the man too much. If they wanted to give him the song, he deserved it.

An hour later, when he came to the studio, I even helped Muddy learn it. I stayed to play back-up guitar. Sure, my heart was hurting, but my heart was also happy that Muddy was getting good material. He did it beautifully, and I'd have to count it among his best records.

All this happened in 1964, and it was surely on my mind when I went back in the studio to sing "My Time After a While." The song said, "It's your turn, baby, but it's gonna be mine after a while." That's how I felt.

Sonny Boy and Little Walter was in the studio that night along with those boys from London they was calling the Rolling Stones, named after one of Muddy's lines. Muddy said they knew more about him than he knew about himself. They had a couple hits that I hadn't heard yet. They were so crazy about Chess Records that they'd come all the way from England to record at 2120. On this night they just came to listen.

First thing they heard was Sonny and Walter arguing.

"I had me this bitch down in Kentucky that was the best pussy of my life," said Walter.

"Where in Kentucky?" asked Sonny Boy.

"Louisville," said Walter.

"Her name Brenda?"

"Yeah."

"I had her too."

"No, you didn't," said Walter. "There be lots of Brendas."

"Is she a heavy-set woman who keeps this black poodle dog around her, even when you be fucking?"

"Matter of fact, she did have her a poodle dog," said Walter.

"Well, sir, let me tell about big Brenda. First thing she got from me was one finger. That didn't make her happy, so I gave her two. When two wouldn't do, you know what I had to give?"

Walter didn't want to ask, but I did.

"What?"

"I give her this"—and then Sonny Boy stuck out his tongue, popped his fingers, and walked out the studio, leaving me and the Rolling Stones rolling on the floor.

The Stones hung around while I recorded "My Time After a While" and afterward gave me some kind words.

Them Stones have always been good to me. Later in my career they came in at just the right time. They paid me big respect, and I give back the same respect. Wasn't for them and other guys like Eric Clapton and Jeff Beck, blues wouldn't have the worldwide recognition it has today. When everyone was singing the praises of the Stones—and the Beatles too—those cats were honest enough to say that it came from Muddy and B. B. and John Lee.

When the Stones came to Chess in '64, they started telling everyone—and even wrote it up in books—that they saw Muddy Waters standing on a ladder where he was whitewashing the walls. They said the Mud had whitewash all over his face. For years Keith Richards repeated this story. His point was that Leonard Chess was using poor Muddy as a handyman.

Leonard and Muddy are long gone, but I was there—and so was Marshall Chess—and we both know this ain't true. If anyone had been used as a handyman, it would have been me. At Chess I was low man in the pecking order, but no one ever asked me to paint walls or mop floors. And if they didn't ask me, they sure as hell wouldn't ask the Mud. Muddy was a proud man. He knew he'd put Chess on the map. He realized his importance. No doubt Leonard cooked the books so that Muddy never got his fair share, but Muddy got something. He had a house. And when he went into that studio, he didn't wear no painter's overalls—he was clean as the board of health. Suit all pressed. Shoes spit-shined polished. Hair processed high and slick. Muddy Waters knew that in Chicago, Illinois, he was boss of the blues. If he wanted to, he could probably have gotten Leonard Chess over to *his* house to whitewash *his* walls. Leonard worked to keep Muddy happy.

As I approached thirty I was happy, but hardly rich. Many a week I'd come up short. That's because the clubs and the record company wasn't paying shit. My father-in-law was yelling for me to get a regular job, and at some point I did. I started driving a tow truck. I wanted to get where I could buy a two-flat house for my family. That couldn't happen if I didn't supplement my low-paying guitar gigs. I had to change my routine: I played my blues till four in the morning and then went to the garage, where I curled up in a corner and slept till 8 a.m. before working till 6 p.m. I stayed on that schedule for years. It was rough, but it did teach me every street and back alley in Chicago.

In the truck and in my house I listened to the radio. I heard the Beatles and the Stones. In their songs I heard echoes of our music. I thought that was good. I felt like we was being appreciated. I also loved Ray Charles singing "Hit the Road, Jack," a song written by the bluesman Percy Mayfield, a great artist himself. When Ray sang country and hit with "I Can't Stop Loving You," I had to smile. Things were expanding. I liked what was happening at Motown. I liked Stevie Wonder blowing his harmonica on "Fingertips." Little Eva's "Locomotion" got me going. So did James Brown's "Night Train." In Chicago a label called Veejay had Jerry Butler doing "He Will Break Your Heart" and Gene Chandler's "Duke of Earl." The Impressions were from Chicago. I loved their "Gypsy Woman" and "It's All Right." When Curtis Mayfield came to see me in Gary, he said how much the loved the blues. We was all connected.

But we was also disconnected. Even the greatest bluesmen—take Muddy or Lightnin', B. B. or John Lee—stand alone. They got their own story to tell, a story no one can tell but them. For a very long time only black people wanted to hear that story. That was fine. There was enough black fans that you could make a dollar or two playing your blues. But here in the sixties black folk was changing their taste. Motown was bringing them a smoother sound. Black folk like smooth. James Brown was bringing it with more dance flavor. Black folk like to dance. Curtis Mayfield had a little message in his music. Black folk like messages. All this meant that, more and more, blacks was listening to blues less and less. And as the sixties moved on, blacks with money started turning their back on the blues altogether.

B. B. tells a story about playing a show with the early Motown acts. The artists gave him respect, but when he was introduced to the all-black crowd, he heard big boos. That got B. B. to crying. He said that his own people looked on him like he was a farmer wearing overalls and smoking a corncob pipe. Meanwhile, he was dressed slick. His band was dressed slick. They was sharp as they could be. But the young blacks saw B. B. as old hat. They saw him as a grandfather playing their grandfather's music. At the time B. B. was thirty-six.

The sixties were confusing. The world was shifting in ways that didn't make a lot to sense to a country boy from Lettsworth, Louisiana. I wanted to keep playing, and I wanted to keep exciting people with what I played. I felt like I was keeping up with the music, and at times I knew I was even ahead of the music.

That made me feel good inside. But it didn't stop me from doing the one thing I could count on—driving that goddamn tow truck all over the city of Chicago.

Brother, Brother

Junior Wells gets his own chapter in my book. He's one of the craziest characters to come running through my life. I'm grateful to God that we hooked up like we did—not that it was all smooth sailing. Junior came with a boatload of baggage, but with Junior by my side, I do believe I raised the stakes. Together we made music I could never have made alone. He inspired me.

I met him at the 708 in the late fifties. He was just a little over a year older than me, but he had a lifetime more experience. Naturally, I knew him as the cat that took Little Walter's place in Muddy's band. That was the only credential he needed. With all them harp men hustling in Chicago and then to be chosen by the Mud—well, he had to be great.

He *was* great, and he'd be the first tell you.

"I studied on the greats when I a little bitty boy in West Memphis," he told me many a time. "First one I heard was the original Sonny Boy Williamson. Never met him, but they'd play him on the radio. When I moved to Chicago in '46, I was eleven. I had me my harp and was ready to go. Then I learned that the original Sonny Boy was killed right here at the Plantation Club. That was like a warning, but hell, I was gonna be a bluesman, danger or no danger. I went right up to Sonny Boy the second—Rice Miller—in a barroom and asked him to show me some tricks on the harmonica. 'Motherfucker,' he said, 'you too dumb and stupid.' He 'bout cut off my head. He told me to get the fuck outta his face. I was the determined kind, so I asked him again. That's when he pulled his blade and told me to get. I got in a hurry.

"But Muddy and Tampa Red were nicer. When I was a teenager, they let me sit in with them at the Ebony Club. Then I had me some trouble. At school a big bully hit me for no reason. So I got me a baseball bat and retaliated upside his head. They was gonna throw me outta school and put me in jail. But at juvenile court Tampa Red and Muddy showed up to testify on my behalf. Said I had talent and a future. Judge made Muddy sign something that said he'd care for me. He did. I walked out a free man. I thanked Muddy and then went off to catch the bus. Muddy said, 'Where you going, Junior? Get in the car with me.' I said, 'I got places to go.' 'The hell you do. I'm in charge of your black ass.' Muddy was blocking my way to the bus, so I gave him a shove. Muddy didn't say nothing. He just pulled out his .25 automatic and pointed it at my head. 'I got no problem with shooting you—no problem at all.' I listened to him. That's when I knew I had a daddy."

Little Walter and Muddy had a falling out over "Juke," Walter's big hit. Walter claimed he never got his share of proper attention and money. Meanwhile, Junior claimed that Walter had stolen the tune from the group he had formed, the Four Aces, with Louis and David Myers and Fred Below. Junior said "Juke" was their theme song.

With Walter gone, Junior became Muddy's new man. Even moved into the Mud's house. That caused some problems. Muddy and his wife Geneva was charging Junior a little rent, but when Junior found out some other musician was staying there free of charge, he went crazy and pulled a knife on Muddy. Muddy didn't blink. He up and smacked Junior's face before Junior had a chance to do anything. Then he grabbed his neck and declared, "I'll fuck up your mouth so bad you'll never play that harp again." That's when Junior backed off. Over the years Junior and Muddy had a father-son love-hate thing.

Muddy told me stories about how he liked to tease Junior. Once they was driving from a gig. Junior and the Mud was in the backseat. Wearing his do-rag, Junior was fast asleep with his mouth wide open. Muddy got a bold idea. He had the driver stop at a grocery store where they bought a small tin of oysters. They opened the can and poured some of the oyster juice into the side of Junior's mouth. Junior kept snoring. The Mud took some of that same juice and poured it over his own dick. Then they shook Junior awake. Junior felt the juice in his mouth and saw the juice on Muddy's prick. Muddy said, "Okay, I'm through. You can go back to sleep." Junior started choking—he was sure Muddy had put his dick in his mouth. Junior went for his knife, but the other cats held him back. When Muddy told the story, he was on the floor laughing.

Another time they was all in a motel. Junior had a gal that fancied Muddy, and Muddy also had a yen for her. So Otis Spann went to Junior's room and said he needed to see Junior in the parking lot.

"Let's talk here," said Junior.

"Parking lot's better," said Otis. "It's a pretty day and we need some fresh air."

They went to the parking lot, where Otis started talking some bullshit. Junior got suspicious, so he headed back to his room. Gal was gone. He started looking around. That's when he heard noises from Muddy's room. Through the window he could see the boss banging his girlfriend. By then Otis and the others had caught up with Junior and kept him from breaking into the room. But they did let him watch.

"The fucked-up thing," said Junior when he told me his version of the story, "was that the bitch was enjoying it even more than Muddy."

Blue Mondays at Theresa's was where the cats came to jam. That's where me and Junior first started in together. Wasn't no formal band. We didn't have no business arrangement or musical arrangements. As a guitar man and harp player, we was just good grits and gravy. After a while you'd hear people say, "Oh, y'all are the new Muddy and Walter."

I didn't like that talk, and I discouraged it. I'm believing that there'll never be a new Muddy and Walter. That's like saying there'll be a new Rosa Parks or a new Martin Luther King Jr. These are pioneers. These are folk who led the way. When Sonny Stitt came around after Charlie Parker, he was in Chicago. We heard him and loved him. But you don't wanna compare Stitt to Parker 'cause Parker carved the new wood. Muddy and Walter carved the new wood. They brought something that wasn't there before. I don't belong in that company. And for all his mighty talent, neither does Junior.

Junior had him a hellacious sound on harp, and he was a helluva singer too. He could dance all over the stage. I'd call him an all-around entertainer. When we started doing shows together, he liked my way of not even being in the club when the band started playing. He got him a 150-foot cord for his amp like I had for my guitar. We'd come marching in from the men's room or the kitchen. Alone, I could cause a sensation that way. With Junior the sensation got bigger.

Junior had a beautiful soul. I remember one night when Sonny Boy dropped by Theresa's—the same Sonny Boy who'd pulled a knife when Junior wanted some advice on how to play. Junior wouldn't even look at him. Sonny Boy tried to say something, but Junior turned his back.

"Wait a minute, motherfucker," said Sonny Boy. "I know you pissed about how I did you."

"Goddamn right I am," said Junior.

"But look here, I told you that shit to see if you was serious. If you really wanted to be a bluesman, I figured you was the kinda cat who would go off and prove me wrong."

"That's just what I did."

"I know," said Sonny Boy. "I hear. So all I'm saying is that I did you a solid. Wasn't for me, you wouldn't blow good as you blow. I got you off your ass, boy."

Junior closed his eyes and didn't say nothing. I could hear the wheels turning inside his head.

"You know something," he told Sonny Boy. "You right."

From then on they was cool.

Like a lot of us, Junior had a tough time with the record companies. He told me how he cut his tune "Hoodoo Man Blues" back in the early fifties with Willie Dixon and Memphis Slim. Junior and the label rep went to a deejay to get it played. The rep slipped the deejay $25, but I guess that wasn't enough 'cause the deejay took the 78 shellac record, threw it on the floor, and smashed it to bits.

"That hurt me to my soul," Junior told me, "until I swore I'd never record that song again."

Another thing about Junior: he had a James Brown complex. He felt that James had stolen his thunder. I think that goes back to "Messin' with the Kid."

"Messin'," came out in 1960 and was Junior's biggest number. He told me—and anyone else who'd listen—how he came up with the idea. A producer named Mel London was set to pick him up for a session at 8 p.m. When Mel got there, Junior's baby daughter Regina was sitting in her little chair watching TV.

"Where's your daddy?" asked Mel.

"Asleep."

"Well, get him up."

"No."

"Why not?"

"He likes to sleep."

"It's time for him to go to work. If you won't wake him up, I will."

"No you won't."

"Careful, kid, or I'll get you too."

Regina looked Mel dead in the eye and said, "You ain't gonna be messin' with the kid."

When Junior got up and drove to the studio with Mel, they were laughing about it. Junior said that phrase gave him the idea for the song, and he put some music and rhymes around it. But London got the writer's credit and handled the copyright. Junior didn't get anything.

The song became popular, and truth be told, it does have a James Brown feeling to it. But you can't say that James flat-out copied Junior. The way music goes, we all borrow from each other, especially blues music. But as James Brown grew into a superstar, Junior felt like he deserved that same spot. He never stopped trying to have him a James Brown–sized hit. Yet he missed the mark. Wasn't that Junior wasn't a great showman—he was. But aside from Jackie Wilson, there ain't ever been a showman like James Brown. James created his own category of funk.

Early on, Junior asked me to go on the road with his band as a sideman. Nothing wrong with that. Junior got to Chicago ten years ahead of me. He'd toured with Muddy's band and I hadn't. I could see myself joining Junior had it not been for the stories. Last one I heard was about Junior being out of town, where he was drinking at a bar when his drummer told him it was time to leave.

"You're fired," said Junior.

"For what?" asked the drummer.

"For disturbing me while I'm drinking."

For a while Dick Waterman, Junior's manager, had to play drums even though Dick had never picked up a drumstick before.

My attitude was simple: jamming with Junior was always good. He stopped where I started and he started where I stopped. Whenever Junior showed up the club, I knew we could burn with a blaze. Sometimes the club owners, knowing that customers liked us playing as a team, put both our names on the bill. That was fine. But going out on the road with Junior had to be more trouble than it was worth.

I was right, but I was also wrong. You'll soon see what I mean.

Flying High, Flying Low

By 1965 Joan and I had our third girl, Colleen Nanette, and was living in the Chicago-style two-flat house I'd bought at 1218 East 72nd Street on the South Side. I wasn't making a cent from selling any records. I sure as hell hadn't turned into a star. I'd get a few dollars backing up other Chess artists in the studio, and I kept working the clubs at night while driving the tow truck during the day. It was a rough routine, so I was happy to break it up the few times I found some gigs in Europe.

I give credit to the bluesmen that played overseas before me. The first ones were Big Bill Broonzy, Josh White, and Lonnie Johnson. Then came Sonny Terry and Brownie McGhee. But when Muddy showed up with Otis Spann, that really opened up the door to what people were calling Chicago blues.

During these trips I met Roy Orbison and got to hang with T-Bone Walker. Willie Dixon got me a few dates in London clubs. That's when I heard talk about this group called the Yardbirds. A young kid named Rod Stewart volunteered to be my valet. He started talking about how England was in love with rhythm and blues. When I see Rod these days, we laugh about how he was driving me around London.

After one gig two cats came backstage and started questioning me like I was the teacher and they was the students. This was the first time I'd hear their names—Eric Clapton and Jeff Beck. They said they slept in a van all night just to get to see me. They also said how they never knew a Strat could play blues. They thought the Strat was only for country music. I told them that it wasn't my idea. I got it from Guitar Slim. All they wanted to hear was stories about Guitar Slim, Lightnin' Slim, and Lightnin' Hopkins. They knew every Chess record where I backed up Muddy and Wolf. They also knew my little single recordings, even the ones I'd done for Cobra.

To make ends meet I had played the gig with only drums and bass. That impressed Clapton. He said, "Man, you make a trio sound big as a full band. And the way you keep your feet moving and throw the guitar around—wow!"

"Ain't nothing," I said, "compared to what I seen Guitar Slim do."

I got on TV on a show called *Ready Steady Go!*, where the announcer called me Chuck Berry. I was also introduced as Chubby Checker.

Germany was another trip altogether. I went over for the American Folk Blues Festival. I understood why Muddy came back from Europe all confused. I got booed because I looked too young, dressed too slick, and my hair was up in a do. Someone said he was also disappointed that I didn't carry no whiskey bottle with me on stage. They thought bluesmen needed to be raggedy, old, and drunk.

During that performance I was sure I was fucking up because I didn't hear a sound from the audience. Wasn't like in America, where folk yell up to you that they're digging it. In England, when I got through, all I got was mild applause.

Then I was criticized for doing James Brown's "Out of Sight." Some writers said a bluesman got no business doing rock and roll or rhythm and blues or whatever they was calling it. Truth is that "Out of Sight" was popular, and I wanted to do something popular. Besides, all this rock and roll and rhythm and blues came out of the blues.

On that same show in Germany when Joe Turner sang "Flip Flop and Fly," one of his big hits with the rock and roll crowd, it was really a straight-up twelve-blues bar. No one complained. So was "Shake, Rattle and Roll." When I played behind Big Mama Thornton doing "Hound Dog," that went over okay. "Hound Dog" was one of the things that got Elvis started—and it was nothin' but the blues.

Far as I saw, blues fans in Europe was mixed up as a motherfucker. They wanted pure blues, when there ain't such thing. Blues always been a gumbo where you throw everything in the pot. Blues ain't no pedigree; it's a mutt. And far as I'm concerned, mutts are beautiful.

The most beautiful thing about those European trips, though, was spending time with two people—Big Mama and John Lee Hooker.

I was in Baden-Baden Germany, upstairs in my room, when I heard all this commotion from down in the lobby. I went down and saw Big Mama, Roosevelt Sykes, Eddie Boyd, and some other guys. Everyone was drinking hot straight whiskey. I couldn't handle that, so I took my guitar, went off into the corner, and started playing "Boogie Chillen."

After a while a skinny man with a deep voice came over and said, "W-w-w-w-w-w-w-w-where'd you learn that?"

"I been knowing it forever," I said.

"B-b-b-b-b-b-b-b-but who t-t-t-t-t-taught it to you?"

"Got it off the record."

"You ain't p-p-p-p-p-p-p-p-p-playing it 'xactly like the r-r-r-r-r-record."

"Who you to say?"

"I can s-s-s-s-s-say it c-c-c-c-c-c-cause that's my s-s-s-s-shit you p-p-p-p-p-playing."

"No, it ain't. It's John Lee's."

"Who the f-f-f-f-f-f-f-f-fuck you think y-y-y-y-y-y-you talkin' to?"

I looked over at the man.

"Don't know," I said.

"I'm J-j-j-j-j-j-j-j-johnny."

"I didn't know John Lee stuttered."

"Like I s-s-s-s-said, you d-d-d-d-d-don't know s-s-s-s-s-s-s-s-s-s-shit."

Ever since then we became the best of friends.

Also became good friends with Big Mama, a woman who wore manly clothes and stood big as a house. During one of those concerts when I was playing "Hound Dog" behind her, her teeth fell out. I didn't know what she'd do. Well, sir, she just bent down, picked up her teeth, and put 'em back in her mouth without missing a lick. She kept on singing, and holy shit, that woman could sing! After that performance I thought maybe I should get me some false teeth, let them fall out while I was playing, and pick 'em up like Big Mama picked up hers.

The rest of the musicians on the tour didn't like hanging out with Big Mama because she was big and bossy. I think her manly ways had them thinking that if they said the wrong thing, she could kick their ass. I believe she could. For some reason she took a liking to me.

One morning I was killing time in the lobby with the other cats, when here comes Big Mama off the elevator. She had on a man's trousers and a big ol' Stetson hat. She came right over to me.

"Buddy Guy," she said, "you and I going souvenir shopping."

Other cats looked at me like I was crazy to go. But what could I do? I liked the lady. Was her business how she dressed. Besides, she was as good a blues singer as Joe Turner—and that's saying something. I couldn't say no. Me and her hit the stores. People looked at us funny. I know we was a strange couple, but I didn't care.

During that same trip we had to ride in the car from city to city. It was the driver, me, Big Mama, and John Lee Hooker. Mama and Johnny didn't get on. She was too bossy for him, and he was too contrary for her. I'd sit there for hours, watching them go at it, all the while laughing my ass off.

This was when I came to love John Lee very deeply. Like a lot of these cats, he was a practical man—he got his money before he gave you his music—but he was also a funny man. He had the best stories of anyone. Part of what made them funny was the country way he told them—that and his stutter and lisp. His stutter made you eager to hear how the story would end.

In Germany we were at a restaurant where he wanted to order a steak. None of us knew no German, and the waiter didn't know English.

"B-b-b-bring me a s-s-s-s-s-steak and sp-sp-sp-sp-spaghetti," John Lee said.

Waiter looked puzzled.

John Lee started making motions with his hands to look a crawling snake. "N-n-n-n-n-noodles," he said. "Y-y-y-y-you know—spaghetti."

Waiter ran to the kitchen and came back with some noodles. John Lee smiled. "O-o-o-o-okay, now cook me a s-s-s-s-s-steak."

Waiter ran back and forth from the kitchen carrying different stuff—a hot dog, a chicken, a piece of fish—but no steak.

"G-g-g-g-g-goddamnit," said John Lee. "I want m-m-m-m-m-me a steak!"

Waiter just shrugged.

John Lee snapped his fingers like he got an idea.

"Okay, m-m-m-m-m-motherfucker," he said, "h-h-h-h-h-here's what I w-w-w-w-w-w-w-want."

John Lee started motioning his fists like he was milking a cow.

Waiter still didn't get it. That's when John Lee took in a deep breath and came out this ear-shattering "M-m-m-m-m-m-m-moooooooooooooooooooo!"

Waiter smiled and John Lee got himself his steak.

After dinner I was hoping he'd start talking about his music. Funny thing, though, how bluesmen don't talk that much about music. They like talking about women.

"W-w-w-w-w-w-w-when I s-s-s-s-s-still down on the farm in M-m-m-m-m-mississippi," John Lee said, "I had me all the girls. Had me f-f-f-f-f-five or six different lil' girls b-b-b-b-b-b-b-because I was the guitar player. Them g-g-g-g-g-girls favor the guitar players. Now one day one of my g-g-g-g-girls, she come running up to me talkin' 'bout, 'J-j-j-j-j-j-johnny, a little boy came by and k-k-k-k-k-k-k-kissed Mary.' M-m-m-m-m-m-mary was one of my girls. Well, I got my switchblade w-w-w-w-with me, and I go d-d-d-d-d-down to the d-d-d-d-ditch where the girls liked to p-p-p-p-p-p-p-play."

On the plantations where me and John Lee worked, they had a ditch to run off the water if it rained too much for the cotton and corn.

"L-l-l-l-l-little midget standing there," said John Lee, "and I s-s-s-say, 'Hey, you kiss m-m-m-m-my girl?' M-m-m-m-midget nods his head like he d-d-d-d-d-d-did. So I p-p-p-p-p-pop him in the face. Would have s-s-s-s-s-s-stuck him with the knife 'cept that I f-f-f-f-felt sorry for him. After I pop him h-h-h-h-h-he don't move, so I pop him again. S-s-s-s-s-s-still don't fall down. Next thing I know he's j-j-j-j-jumping up on my chest and b-b-b-b-beating on me so hard until m-m-m-m-my girls are yelling at m-m-m-m-m-me 'Get him, Johnny, g-g-g-get him!' But this g-g-g-g-g-goddamn midget is whopping me until he whoops all the c-c-c-c-clothes off me. I'm here to tell you, B-b-b-b-buddy, them things are strong. D-d-d-d-don't you ever jump on no m-m-m-m-m-m-midget."

John Lee had stories of his country life along with stories about his city life.

"When I f-f-f-f-first gets to Detroit," he said, "I was pretty l-l-l-l-loose with my knife. Folk knew I w-w-w-w-wouldn't take no shit. I was p-p-p-p-playing at the Henry Swing Club with my g-g-g-g-girl cousin s-s-s-s-sitting close when I l-l-l-l-l-look up and see her b-b-b-b-b-boyfriend p-p-p-p-p-p-punch her face with his f-f-f-fist. Well, I stop playing and g-g-g-go for my knife, and they h-h-h-h-h-hustle him out the club, and I'm w-w-w-w-wanting to go after him. By the time we g-g-g-g-g-get outside, h-h-h-h-he's across the street, and my friends, they h-h-h-h-holding me back 'cause my blade is out and they sayin' to the c-c-c-c-cat across the street, 'We holding him, we trying to h-h-h-h-hold him back,' but I was r-r-r-ready to r-r-r-r-run over to that m-m-m-m-m-motherfucker and cut him when, under the streetlight, I s-s-s-s-s-see something shiny, some blue steel shining. I s-s-s-s-s-s-see that the c-c-c-c-c-c-c-cat's holding a .38 automatic in his h-h-h-h-hand. That's when I s-s-s-say, 'Fellas, you don't w-w-w-w-w-worry 'bout holding me back 'cause I done cooled off, and I'm g-g-g-g-gonna go back inside to p-p-p-p-p-p-play my g-g-g-g-guitar."

Both me and John Lee knew Willie Dixon real well. Willie didn't have no high opinion of John Lee's songwriting. I did. I love the songs he made up, but Willie called them simpleminded. One time Willie told Johnny just how he felt.

"Your songs ain't no good," said Willie. "They don't even rhyme."

"Makes n-n-n-n-no d-d-d-d-d-difference," said John Lee.

"Sure it does. They ain't even real songs."

"Oh yeah? Then why do p-p-p-p-p-people b-b-b-b-b-b-buy 'em?"

John Lee waited for an answer, but Willie just walked away.

Riding around Germany, John Lee couldn't stop telling stories.

"Shit, Johnny," said Big Mama, "we done heard enough of your bullshit. Way you be stumbling and stammering, takes forever to get 'em out."

"W-w-w-w-w-what's the b-b-b-b-b-big h-h-h-h-hurry?" asks John Lee.

"I'm just tired of you running your mouth."

"Well, this n-n-n-n-next story has to do with s-s-s-s-s-something that I know you l-l-l-l-l-l-like."

"What's that?" asked Big Mama.

"P-p-p-p-p-p-p-pussy."

Even Big Mama had to laugh. Then, like me, she leaned in to listen.

"S-s-s-s-s-starts out with w-w-w-w-with me and Jimmy Reed playing a show in Detroit. After the g-g-g-g-g-gig we both got sloppy d-d-d-d-d-drunk and picked up two w-w-w-w-w-women who w-w-w-w-wanted us real bad. The four of us g-g-g-go to a motel and g-g-g-g-get us two r-r-r-r-rooms. Me and my g-g-g-g-gal got the upstairs room, J-j-j-j-j-jimmy and his bitch got the one downstairs. I had a hundred d-d-d-d-d-d-dollars in my p-p-p-p-p-pocket that I wasn't about to l-l-l-l-l-l-lose. Now I'm gonna f-f-f-f-f-fuck this woman until she ain't ever gonna wanna s-s-s-s-s-see me no more, but I'm also g-g-g-g-gonna keep my money. So when she ain't l-l-l-l-l-l-l-looking, I put my money between the b-b-b-b-b-box spring and the m-m-m-m-m-m-mattress. Well, we get to f-f-f-f-f-fucking real g-g-g-g-g-good and then naturally afterward I f-f-f-f-f-fall to sleep. When I w-w-w-w-w-wake up, the box spring is on t-t-t-t-t-top of me and the b-b-b-b-b-bitch is gone. Ain't b-b-b-b-b-bad enough that she r-r-r-r-run off with my money, but also she done took all my c-c-c-c-c-clothes. All she l-l-l-l-l-leaves me with is my b-b-b-b-b-boxer shorts. So I go r-r-r-r-r-running into the hallway in nothing but my b-b-b-b-b-b-boxers, screaming after her. I look at the b-b-b-b-b-b-bottom of the stairs, and there's Jimmy R-r-r-r-r-reed. He in his b-b-b-b-b-boxer shorts too, looking for his b-b-b-b-bitch, who also done run off. I shout d-d-d-d-d-down at him, 'What h-h-h-h-h-happened to you, m-m-m-m-motherfucker?' He l-l-l-l-l-l-looks up at me and y-y-y-y-y-yells, 'Same thing that happened t-t-t-t-t-to you, Johnny. We both got f-f-f-f-f-f-f-f-f-f-fucked."

Something else happened that same year—1965—that folks still talking about today. I went in the studio for the first time with Junior Wells to record not just a single but a whole album that became known as *Hoodoo Man Blues*.

Junior called and said, "You know this cat Bob Koester?"

"No," I said.

"He's been coming 'round the clubs. He got his own label, Delmark. You heard of it?"

I hadn't.

"He says he wanna record me the way I need to be recorded."

"How's that?"

"He says I don't need no Willie Dixon or no one like that. He wants me to pick whoever I want to play with. He wants me to choose whatever tunes I want. He says the songs don't gotta end after three minutes like a record usually do."

"Will he give you any money?"

"A little."

"Sounds okay, Junior."

"Will you play on it?"

"Will he give me any money?"

"A little."

"Who else you getting?"

"Jack Myers."

"He's a good bass man."

"And Bill Warren on drums."

"No piano?" I asked.

"Don't think so."

"How come?"

"Less cats, more money. You in?"

"I'm in. You already picked out the songs?"

"I'll do it when I get there," said Junior. "Koester wants me to do 'Hoodoo Man Blues.' Says it's the best thing I ever done. But I ain't doing it, so don't even ask me."

"Do as you like. It's your session."

"Damn right."

When I showed up, Bob Koester took me aside and said, "We should try to get Junior to do 'Hoodoo Man Blues.' It'll help sell the album."

"Junior gonna do what Junior gonna do," I said.

"I know that," Bob said, "but if there's an opening and you start into the song, Junior might get the spirit and sing along. I'll have the tape rolling just in case."

First off, Junior wanted to do "Snatch It Back and Hold It," a song he wrote in the James Brown bag. His lyrics even talk about how "I ain't got no brand new bag." This was Junior trying to compete with James.

When we did "Hound Dog," I was thinking of Big Mama Thornton—except that Junior did it his own way until I forgot the original. We did Sonny Boy's "Good Morning, Little Schoolgirl" and a Junior song, "In the Wee Wee Hours." At some point we were pretty loose and Junior was pretty happy, so I started saying how it's been so long since I heard his "Hoodoo Blues Man." I even forgot how it went. That got Junior to start singing it.

"Oh no, Buddy," he said, "I know what y'all are trying to get me to do."

"Well, if it feel good, Junior," I said, "go on and do it."

The spirit came in the room, and we ran it down. Before we started, though, my amp busted, and I had to plug in through the Leslie speaker of a Hammond B3 organ. The sound came out strange, but I've always liked strange. It's a guitar-marries-the-organ sound. Junior heard the sound and smiled. "Hey man," he said, "why not?"

Koester didn't raise no objections. Fact is that Koester didn't say much of anything. He let me and Junior run the show. Never told us how to play or when to cut off a song. Was my first experience of doing a full-length album in one shot.

When it was time to release it, Koester said there were some problems between me and Chess. Said I wasn't allowed to play on another label without their permission.

"Fuck it," I said. "Just put some other name on it."

I knew the little up-front money was the only money I'd ever see.

So the album said, "Junior Wells with the Friendly Chap."

Some forty-seven years later my name is on the cover and the thing is still selling. They call it one of the classic blues records of all time. I can't vouch for that, but it did cement something between me and Junior. Made us realize that as a musical unit, we was tight. Left to our devices, we could burn.

Even though other labels would put me and Junior in the studio again, and even though we did good stuff, nothing was as good as *Hoodoo Man Blues.* They say you gotta capture lightning in a bottle, but with music that might happen only once in a lifetime.

As the sixties marched on, my own life ground to a halt. I was turning thirty, still young, still getting beautiful compliments from the folks in the clubs and a few rock and rollers in England, but I still wasn't able to support my family on music alone.

I was still driving the tow truck, fixing flat tires and changing batteries, working the streets of Chicago every day until I had the map of that sprawling city—south, west, north, and east—planted deep inside my brain. Part of me wanted a change, something to let me be a full-time musician. But another part of me—the cautious part—said that a steady job was better than no job at all.

If something was going to change all that, I sure as hell didn't see it coming.

The Creeper

"Someone here to see you, Buddy," said my boss. I was working in the service department of Litsinger, second biggest Ford dealer in Chicago.

"Tell him I'm on the creeper under this here city truck. Tell him to wait."

"He says it's important."

"Well, if he wants to talk to me while I'm on my back, draining the oil out of this truck, fine."

I kept draining when I saw a pair of feet moving toward me.

"How come you're using a creeper?" asked the stranger. "Can't you put the truck on a lift? Wouldn't that be easier?"

"Sure would," I said, "except this truck's too big for a lift."

"I see."

"You come 'round here to discuss trucks?" I asked.

"No, I came here to discuss music. My name's Dick Waterman, and I manage Junior Wells. I think I can manage you as well. I think I can get you work. I know I can get you work with Junior."

"I've heard Junior mention you, Dick Waterman, but I ain't interested."

"Why not?"

"First off, I've been getting my own club work at night, and I don't need to pay an agent. An agent means less money for me. Second, Junior's always firing his band and stranding them out there on the road. I don't need that kind of aggravation."

"But wouldn't you rather make your money playing music than working at this garage?" asked Waterman.

"I work at this garage 'cause it's honest work. I work 'cause I'm not gonna beg or steal to feed my family. I don't mind working here during the day. I play my music at night."

"You got to be tired at night."

"Mister," I said, "I been working since I was a little boy. When you out there in the field picking cotton under that blistering Louisiana sun, garage work don't seem so bad. Then at night the music lifts me up."

"How much are you making here?" asked Waterman.

"Two dollars an hour."

"That's low pay and dangerous work. You could have an accident and lose a finger."

"But if I'm out there starving to death, I could lose my life."

"I can guarantee you more than two dollars an hour. Matter of fact, I'll write a postdated check that will cover a whole year of work at twice that amount."

"What am I going to do if at the end of the year I go to cash your postdated check and it bounces like a rubber ball?"

Waterman had to laugh.

"It won't bounce. And from what I hear, business in the blues clubs isn't all that good."

I couldn't argue. Black folks were running over to the Regal to hear the Isley Brothers rather than walk down the street to hear some blues. Just a few nights before Waterman showed up I played in front of exactly six people. I played like there was six hundred, but I couldn't help but be a little down.

"This will bring you up," said Waterman. "This will take you where you need to be."

"Tell you what," I said. "I'll try it for two weeks. I'll tell my boss that I'm experimenting with you booking me, but to hold my job. That okay?"

"That's fine. You'll see for yourself. There's an audience for you out there."

Turned out that the audience was white. Our first gig, where I used my buddy A. C. Reed on sax, was the Canterbury House in Ann Arbor. It was filled with students from the University of Michigan. Feeling nervous, I took a few drinks first, then we went out there and exploded. Kids went nuts. We played so hard that, tripping over each other, we actually fell on our faces. That made the college kids love us even more.

Out in the audience someone yelled out, "Hey man, you play Hendrix? Did Hendrix get his shit from you?"

"Who's Hendrix?" I asked.

"You haven't heard of Jimi Hendrix?" he wanted to know.

"No."

"Sounds to me like he's been taking your records to bed with him."

Next up was the Mariposa Folk Festival in Toronto. I was on the bill with Joni Mitchell, Tom Rush, and Richie Havens—names that were new to me. The scene in Toronto was Ann Arbor times a thousand. Must have been thirty thousand people out there, almost all white.

When we arrived, someone said, "This is the real Buddy Guy."

I asked, "Who's the fake Buddy Guy?"

"Some guy Junior Wells has been playing with. Everyone's been talking about that *Hoodoo Man Blues* record. Blues fans know you're on that with him. So he's been saying you're in his band.

"I'll be damned," I said, more amused than angry.

Later I found out that the "fake" Buddy Guy who Junior had been using was Lefty Dizz.

Toronto was wild. I was wild. I used my shoe to strike the guitar and my white handkerchief to pick the strings. I jumped off the stage and had the fans carry me around like I had been elected president of the United States. I even climbed up the light tower where the operator had the spotlight and played from up there. Didn't know what else to do, so I took off my shirt and started unbuckling my pants when the light switched off and the fans screamed like I was the pied piper leading them to glory.

Last gig was in Boston at Club 47, and that turned out good too.

Time I got back to Chicago, the fact was clear: white people was paying good money to hear blues, especially *young* white people. Around this time they started calling kids with long hair hippies. The girls weren't wearing no bras, and everyone was talkin' 'bout free love. I liked that concept. Hippies also liked smoking weed. When they got high, they said the blues sounded better. Because the blues was raw and, like them, didn't give a shit about the establishment, hippies loved them some blues.

With this new feeling of hope, I told my boss at Litsinger Ford that I'd work there only long enough to train my replacement. He understood, and within a month I was gone. Ever since then I've made it on music and music alone.

Dick Waterman, who helped Bonnie Raitt get started, was also helping some of the old Delta blues singers. It was Dick who brought back Son House. Son House meant a lot to me because he meant a lot to Muddy. He was one of the cats Muddy learned from. Muddy had nothing but love for the man.

Waterman had been looking for Son for a long while when he found him—not in a corner of the Delta, but in Rochester, New York. Dick became his manager and brought him out on the road.

Me and Son House was booked on the same show in California. I hadn't met him yet, but when I got back to my motel room, Waterman had left me a note that said, "Don't go to Son House's room. Don't give Son House any drink under any condition."

I was tired, so I started into napping when I heard the sound of an acoustic guitar from the next room. Sounded mighty pretty. Man was singing too, singing one of them Delta blues that make you think of your mama. Had to be Son House. Ignoring Dick's instructions, I got up, grabbed my guitar, and went next door. I had to meet Son. He was a beautiful cat who was happy to hear me say how much Muddy loved him. He started playing a deep blues about a death letter until tears rolled down my face. I felt like Son House was my uncle or my daddy.

I saw he'd been drinking—there was an open bottle on the dresser—but I didn't care. I was so happy to be playing with him. The easy way his fingers picked the strings and the sweet honey pouring out of his voice let you know that he'd been at this his whole life. At this point I'd guess Son was pushing seventy.

When Waterman got back and saw Son had been drinking, he flew into a rage. He figured I gave him the whiskey.

"No, sir," I said. "Didn't give him nothing."

"Well, I packed his bag and checked it twice before we came out here," said Dick. "I know there were no bottles in there."

"You should have checked *your* suitcase," Son said slyly. "I done hid it in there."

Dick wasn't happy, but I was laughing. When Son left the room, I had to tell Dick, "Look, these older cats have always played for a drink and maybe the chance to lay down with a lady. You can't change their ways. Might as well give 'em the pleasure they earned."

In 1966 Willie Dixon called me to the Chess studio for a session on Koko Taylor, a blues singer from Memphis who'd been around Chicago a number of years. Leonard was eager to cut a hit on the lady. He had me, my drummer Fred Below, bassman Jack Myers, and Lafayette Leake on piano, plus a couple of horns. Willie wanted Koko to sing a song that he'd written and recorded on Howlin' Wolf, "Wang Dang Doodle." The story was about a gang of characters—Automatic Slim, Razor Totin' Jim, Butcher Knife Totin' Nancy, Fast Talkin' Fannie—who were about to throw a wang dang doodle of a party. The Wolf didn't have a hit on it, but Willie figured that if he changed up the groove and guitar lines, Koko could make it work.

He asked me if I had any ideas, and I did. Found a way for the guitar to talk to the bass that added a funky flavor. Willie thought I gave it a new snap and stepped out of the way to let me produce the session. Koko sang the shit out of it. Turned into one of the biggest hits Chess had ever seen. At the time I didn't know nothing about producer credit or producer money, and no one—not Willie or Leonard—was about to educate me.

At the same time, English groups like Cream started having hits. The distorted fuzz tones I'd been fucking with for years was all the rage in England. Now that stuff was selling in America. Leonard's son Marshall was still trying to get his old man to let me loose on records, but the name of the Chess show was still *father knows best*.

Leonard was cordial to me, but it wasn't like I ever saw the inside of his house or even the inside of his office. I was just a cat he could count on for sessions. Far as my singles went, I didn't have no big hits. So Leonard wrote me off. That's why I was surprised when Marshall called me up to say his daddy wanted to see me. I knew it wasn't to give me no royalties.

"Buddy," said Leonard Chess as he sat behind his office, "I'm a proud man."

I didn't say nothing. I knew that was true.

"I'm particularly proud," he went on to say, "of my judgment in music. It's been pretty good over the years. I'm also proud of my work in the studio. I've always thought I knew what I was doing."

I still didn't know what he was getting at.

"But when it came to you, I was wrong."

"How do you mean?" I asked.

"I held you back. I said you were playing too much. I thought you were too wild in your style."

I had to smile, but I kept quiet.

"But now I'm seeing these records coming over from England, Buddy, with these groups that are selling millions. And their guitars are even louder and wilder than yours!"

Now I had to break out laughing.

"American groups are starting to copy the English who are really just copying you."

"I'm not the only one they copying," I said.

"Doesn't matter," said Leonard. "Here's what I want you to do."

He got up and came round his desk, looked me in the eye, and said, "I'm gonna bend over so you can kick my ass."

Now I was howling. I wished I had a photograph of this shit. Man, Leonard Chess was asking me to kick his ass!

I was laughing too hard to kick anyone. Besides, it was enough to hear the man admit he was wrong. What came next, though, really surprised me.

"Next record you do here," he said, "you do it your way—not my way. You do it any way you see fit."

"I'm afraid I'm not going to do another record here," I said.

"Why?"

"Because whatever little contract we had done run out. And another company called Vanguard just gave me a check for fourteen hundred dollars to record for them."

"Are you kidding?"

"I'm serious as sin. I deposited the check, and it's done cleared. Chess was a great school for me, and I'm grateful, but graduation day has come and gone. I'm ready to move on."

Daddy's Eyes

When my father came to Chicago, it was the middle of the sixties. I got him to come not because of music but because of baseball. He wanted to see his hero, Don Drysdale, pitch in person. There was a series coming up in Wrigley Field between the Cubs and Dodgers.

"Dodgers gonna pitch Drysdale?" my father asked when I called him down in Baton Rouge.

"Daddy, you know the rotation good as me. It's a three-game series, so there's a good chance he will."

"And if he don't?"

"You'll see Sandy Koufax."

"Koufax ain't as good as Drysdale. Don't have the power."

"Koufax is better," I argued. "He's got the finesse. He's the best since Robin Roberts."

"You can't prove that by me."

"I don't need to prove nothing, Daddy. I just want you to see Chicago."

Seeing Chicago through my father's eyes was great. He saw a good side of the city because I put him in my house, let him play with his grandchildren, and drove him around to all the sights.

Naturally, he wanted to hear me play; he was proud to see people who knew my name and applauded my music. I took him by Chess, introduced him to Muddy and the Wolf, and gave him all the love and attention he deserved. But nothing I did for him could compare to when we walked into Wrigley Field. I could see his eyes soaking it all in.

"It's a small park," he said, looking around. "Yes sir, a small park but a mighty pretty park. I've been seeing it in black and white on the television. Now here it is in color. And there's Ernie Banks. My, my, my."

He surprised me that trip by how he learned the Bible. Knew every part of that book, Old and New. You'd ask him about any character, and Daddy could tell you what part he played in the story. With little education, the man had educated himself deeply when it came to religion.

"Why?" I asked him.

"Think about it, son," he said. "This book's been around and read by millions of people in every language you can think of. Can't say the same about any other book. That means something. Means that the book's got something to teach us."

"And what's that?"

"That there's more to this life than the flesh on our bones. That flesh is gonna fail, son. But something else is gonna live. Talkin' 'bout the spirit. My spirit can't never die. It keeps coming back on me and on you and on everyone I love. You remember that when I'm gone."

In 1967, as he turned fifty-seven, Daddy's heart gave out. A year later, at age sixty-three, my mother, who had lived with her stroke for so many years, followed him to that place where you don't grow old. If the technology in medicine had been offered them like it's been offered me, maybe they could have lived longer. I believe they were satisfied to live long enough to see their kids raised right. They taught us decency, they showered us with love, and they had us believing that God is real as rain.

After my folks were gone I brought my brother Phil up to Chicago. Phil lived there, where he had a good career as a guitarist, respected by everyone. Beyond his talent as a player, Phil could sing nearly good as Otis Redding, his idol.

Junior Wells went around saying that James Brown idolized him, and maybe that was true. Junior could put on a show. After *Hoodoo Man Blues* showed the world what we could do together, Dick Waterman kept after me to form a permanent band with Junior.

"*Permanent* is a strong word," I told Dick.

"Well, how's *temporarily permanent?*" he asked.

"Better. But only with one condition."

"What's that, Buddy?"

"We use my band, not his."

"I don't think he'll object."

"Don't matter if he does," I said, "because that's the only way I'm doing it. If it's my band, he can't fire nobody—not even me. All he can do is quit."

Dick laughed and said, "I see your point."

"Let's hope Junior does too."

He did—and the Buddy Guy/Junior Wells show, with too many stops and starts to count, went on for some twenty years.

There were really two Juniors: one when he was sober and the other when he was drunk. Sober Junior would give you the shirt off his back and the last dollar in his wallet. Sober Junior was a sweetheart. Drunk Junior was a different deal. He could get ornery, mean, and downright evil.

Strange part is that these two Juniors split up into another two people—the Junior before he got stabbed and the Junior after the stabbing.

The stabbing happened toward the end of the sixties. Before that the State Department sent him to Vietnam to entertain the troops. Junior did great over there. Pictures of him and Hubert Humphrey came out in *Ebony* magazine. He was feeling all good about himself. He was feeling respected.

Then came the stabbing. Terrible as it was, the incident made me love him more because it made me feel for him more. It broke my heart to see him so changed.

It happened at Pepper's Lounge at three in the morning. I wasn't there, but they called me right away.

Junior was at Pepper's when his then-girlfriend, a married woman, came up from behind him and put a knife in his back. She lunged it in so deep that it punctured his lungs. The reason for the attack was crazy. The woman, who was two-timing her husband, was told by friends that Junior was two-timing her. These so-called friends said that Junior was with his "other woman" down at Pepper's. Junior had had some kids with this "other woman," but the truth was that Junior didn't even know that the "other woman" was in the club. Besides, he'd broken up with the "other woman" a long time ago. But the stabbing woman didn't bother to ask no questions—she went for blood and she got it.

When I got to the hospital, Junior was conscious and wanted to leave. He wanted to go home and go to sleep. The doctors said that, although the puncture wasn't deep, he could start bleeding internally. If that happened, he might never wake up. They needed him to stay. Somehow—don't ask me how—I convinced the stubborn man to listen to the doctors. He stayed and survived and, at first, seemed to bounce back to normal. But Junior would never know normal again. That stabbing aggravated his soul. He became an angry man, and when his anger got mixed with liquor, there was hell to pay.

I'm not saying that Junior didn't continue to play great—he did. Me and him was ham and eggs. But it didn't take much for his eggs to get scrambled, burning up my ham and scorching the frying pan.

Before I signed with Vanguard, I was up in Toronto playing a gig when Dick Waterman called.

"The Beatles want to sign you," he said.

"Sign me to what?" I asked.

"Apple Records. That's their label."

I was flattered that the Beatles knew my music well enough to offer me a contract, but I had to know the terms.

"The upfront money is decent," said Waterman.

"Tell them what I really want is a house. My two-flat is getting small for my family."

"I'll tell them."

Next day Waterman called again.

"They'll buy the house," he said.

"Great. I'll sign."

"You can live in the house, but they'll own it."

"That ain't no good."

"Why not?"

"'Cause they can kick me out whenever they wanna. *I* wanna own the house."

"I'll tell them."

He did, but they wouldn't go for it. My deal with the Beatles was over before it began.

That song I like so well called "Money" says that your loving gives me such a thrill, but your love don't pay no bills. Well, even if it didn't pay no bills, I got me a big thrill when John Lee Hooker called me in 1967 and said, "B-b-b-b-b-b-b-buddy G-g-g-g-g-g-guy, how you feel 'bout p-p-p-p-p-playing on my record?"

"Johnny," I said, "I feel great."

Song was called "The Motor City Is Burning"—all about the terrible riots that messed up Detroit.

Many people say it's hard to play with John Lee because he changes up the tempo and adds verses without telling you. I had no trouble, and I'll you why. I put my chair right in front of him so we could play face to face. I let him know with my eyes and my fingers that he didn't have to worry about nothing. I was there to follow him. Didn't matter to me if he changed the beat twelve times and added six new verses. I was with him. Man, I was thrilled for him to lead the way. As he sang about how the Big D was on fire, how his hometown was burning down to the ground, how it was worse than Vietnam, I could see the scenes. I could see that this man was a real poet. He painted pictures of real life. He was letting us see the soldiers on the streets of Detroit, flames everywhere, the feeling of panic, the confusion in his brain. He wasn't worried about whether the words rhymed or how long the song lasted. He was free—freer than any bluesman who ever done played.

A friend once explained to me how modern painters like Picasso were free to paint whatever they felt. If the lines was crooked or a woman had three eyes, didn't matter. Well, that was John Lee. He was a modern painter of the burning blues.

When we got through recording "The Motor City Is Burning," I was exhausted but happy, like I had just got through running up stairs or having heavy sex.

John Lee was all smiles. He looked at me and said, "B-b-b-b-b-buddy G-g-g-g-g-guy, you can p-p-p-p-p-play with me a-a-a-a-a-a-anytime."

"Anytime you call, Johnny, I'll come a-running."

Turned out to be the only record we ever made together—but that's okay. It's a jewel.

My first record came out on Vanguard in 1968, *A Man and Blues*. I was blessed to have Otis Spann on piano and Wayne Bennett on rhythm guitar along with my favorites, Jack Myers on bass and heartbeat-steady Fred Below on drums. I couldn't be happier getting an advance—my first for any record—but I wasn't all that happy with Samuel Charters, the producer. Charters, like the cats who found Muddy in the Delta, was a blues purist. He was a blues scholar, which is a beautiful thing—beautiful to have cats writing down the history and preserving it in museums. But at age thirty-two, I didn't feel like a museum piece. I was still a young man looking to kick plenty of ass. Charter wasn't all that different than Leonard Chess. He had *his* notion of what the blues should be. He wanted that clean sound that so many producers think make for a good blues record. I still wanted to explode like I did when I played live—but that ain't what Charters wanted.

I liked the money and I liked that I was cutting LPs under my name, so I caved in. Nothing wrong with these Vanguard records—a lot of people like them—but I still felt like I held back.

That year, 1968, was marked by death, none more painful to me than my mom's.

In April Martin Luther King Jr. was murdered. Wasn't a black person in America—and millions of whites—who didn't take that personally. It was like your father or uncle or big brother had been killed—and for no right reason. I can't say that I could have marched with Dr. King because I'm one of those fools without the wisdom to turn the other cheek. I would have struck back and ruined everything. But I admired his plan. I knew it was Godly. And I saw it working.

Come June Bobby Kennedy was gunned down in Los Angeles. This wave of shootings—starting in 1963 when Medgar Evers and President Kennedy were killed and continuing into 1965 when Malcolm X was murdered—had us believing we was living in a land of violence.

On the blues front you'd have to call Little Walter a violent man. He didn't hold back on his temper. Fact is that he never held back on anything—his playing, drinking, gambling, or women. He had scars from to head to foot, and he was ready to cut anyone he didn't like. That was just his way. He kept his feelings right in front of his face. Maybe that's why he was the baddest harp man who ever done slipped one of those things in his mouth.

Ran into Little Walter in the streets one day. It was morning time and I had just got through playing one of those early sets at Theresa's.

"Hey, motherfucker," he said, "you seen my lady?"

"Yes," I said. "She's in the club with her mama."

"She was supposed to have food on the table for me. I got home and there wasn't shit. I'm going in there to kick her ass."

"Wouldn't do that, Walter. Her mama's big as the side of a barn and strong as a mule. Her mama ain't gonna let you whip no one."

"I got a plan," he said. "But first I need a drink."

"Well, go ahead and get one."

"I need you to buy me a pint."

I thought to myself, *This is coming from a guy who had the biggest record—"Juke"—you'd ever want to hear.* Of course that was many years ago. He'd been through hard times. He'd gotten shot and he walked with a limp.

I bought him the pint.

"Now, Buddy, I want you to go in there and help me whip their asses."

"No, sir," I said.

"You scared?"

"Hell, yes, I'm scared. Both those ladies are beasts."

"They ain't that mean," he said.

"Mean enough."

"Lookee here, Buddy, we bluesmen gotta stick together."

"Yes," I said, "when it comes to music. But not when it comes to getting beat up by two angry bitches."

"So I gotta do it myself?" he asked.

"I wouldn't do it at all."

"You don't think I can whup 'em?"

"That woman as much as sits on you, Walter, and you might not get up again."

"Watch me."

I stayed by the door as Walter marched in and went right up to the booth where his lady and her mama were sitting. He started cussing them 'bout how he was hungry and expected food on the table. They cussed him back 'bout how he can get his own damn food.

"Fuck you both!" he screamed.

That's when he took the package of salt and pepper he'd been holding in his hand and threw it in their eyes. Before they knew what was happening, he was punching them both in the face. By the time they were able to dilute their eyes with water, he had done limped out and was long gone.

The last days of Little Walter were sad. In the winter of 1968 I heard the story from Junior.

"I seen Walter down there around Theresa's," said Junior, "shooting dice on the street, not far from that apartment where he was living. Cat threw the dice, but he threw 'em at Walter's butt. The dice came up with the winning combination, but Walter said it wasn't fair—you couldn't roll the dice against no one's ass and call it a winner. When the cat reached for the money, Junior grabbed it first. Then the cat took a hammer and hit Walter upside the head. Walter seemed to take the blow okay. Didn't even fall. But he was shocked enough to where the cat took the money. Walter went home and told his old lady he had a headache. He needed to get in the bed and sleep. Well, his old lady didn't think nothing of it. Just gave him aspirin with a glass of water. He fell right asleep. In the morning he was dead. Come to find out it was a concussion. He was bleeding from the inside. Hemorrhaged to death."

There were other stories about how he died, but Junior swore he saw it with his own eyes. You could say a lot of things about the short life of Little Walter. He died at age thirty-seven. Like me, he was born in Louisiana and found himself trying to cope with the crazy blues life of Chicago. Unlike me, though, he started something new. He invented something new. They say that King Oliver and Louis Armstrong invented the jazz trumpet. They say Jelly Roll Morton invented the jazz piano. They say Charlie Christian invented the jazz guitar. They say Coleman Hawkins, Lester Young, and Charlie Parker invented the jazz saxophone. In that same breath you gotta say Little Walter invented the blues harmonica. No one had that sound before him. No one could make the thing cry like a baby and moan like a woman. No one could put pain in the harp and have it come out so pretty. No one understood that the harmonica—just as much as a trumpet, a trombone, or a saxophone—could have a voice that would stop you in your tracks, where all you could say was, "Lord, have mercy."

Far as his career went, he went up early and then kept going down. You can look at B. B., Muddy, and John Lee and wonder why Walter, who had as much talent, never found the money success they did. Those guys had promoters, of course, who helped build their popularity. Walter never found a promoter who could do that for him. Was it because Walter was too tough to work with, or was it because promoters didn't understand how great he was? Or was it just luck? B. B. and Muddy and John Lee had good fortune. Walter didn't.

In music some of the most talented people die penniless while some of the least talented get rich as Rockefeller. Bad habits have a lot to do with it. But so does bad luck. And when you got both, the odds are against you. With my own eyes I seen that happen to two people I met along the way—Jimi Hendrix and Janis Joplin.

"Who the Hell Are These Guys?"

In 1967, the year before Little Walter died, me and Junior Wells were invited to the Newport Folk Festival. This goes back to Muddy going in years earlier, knocking out the crowd and knocking down the doors so other blues acts could walk on in.

When we arrived, someone said that, aside from performing, we were expected to conduct an afternoon "workshop." When I asked what that that meant, the man said, "It's where you play and talk about how you make your music. People can ask you questions. It's very informal and gives the fans a chance to understand why you do what you do."

Sounded good to me.

"How many people turn up for these things?" I asked.

"A few dozen. We put you in a tent and set up folding chairs."

Me and Junior got there early to set up. Turned out that the tent was already filled with people, so they had to move us to a giant-sized tent. That got filled up in a hurry. People were standing everywhere. In the end, where some of the other workshops had as many as a hundred fans, ours had thousands.

George Wein, the fellow who ran the festival, ran around saying, "Who the hell are these guys?"

He had never heard of Buddy Guy and Junior Wells—but the fans had.

That same year I was booked into the Avalon Ballroom in San Francisco. This was my first real taste of the hippie scene. I didn't go looking for any these hippie bands, but they found me. Jefferson Airplane, for example, called me to open their shows.

I was a little nervous before playing the Avalon. The white hippie musicians liked me, but would their fans follow? Did they want me to play Tex Ritter songs? Did they want rock and roll? Couldn't be sure. I wasn't about to take no chances, so I lit up the Avalon. I gave 'em my best balls-out Guitar Slim show. I was hanging from the rafters, blasting my shit until all them hippies looked like they were climaxing from good sex.

Sex was on my mind because of all the free-love talk. I found me a couple of hippie chicks during that trip and had a nice taste of what they'd been talking about. Yes, sir, I didn't see nothing wrong with no free love.

My hit with the hippies got me booked into New York. I was excited because it was my first time playing the big city. The joint was called the Scene, and the Chamber Brothers were on the bill with me. God knows what I did that night—played the guitar between my legs, over my back, on top of my head.

During a break Waterman said, "Hendrix is here. He wants to tape you. He wants to jam with you."

I remember hearing Hendrix's name from that time in Toronto, but I still wasn't all that sure who he was. Hadn't heard no records by him and didn't know what the fuss was about.

"Sure," I said. "Let him record. Let him jam."

He came in with a reel-to-reel recorder that he set up in front of the bandstand. Can't remember the song we did, but he joined in with no problems. Said he was used to being in the background. He had a wild look but a shy manner. When it was time for him to solo, I heard him as a good bluesman who, like me, went looking for new sounds and didn't mind if he got a little lost along the way. He had a wah-wah pedal and used it to make certain points. Earl Hooker had that pedal earlier, but Hendrix leaned on it much heavier than Earl did. I could hear that Hendrix was something else.

After the set he thanked me.

"You're one of my teachers," he said.

I was flattered, but I couldn't remember getting paid for any lessons. I wished him luck and never saw him again.

Our first white fans were musicians who came to the black side of Chicago and sat in. Michael Bloomfield, Paul Butterfield, Steve Miller, and Elvin Bishop were some of those cats leading the early charge. When they got famous with bands of their own, they never forgot us. They told the press, "Listen to Muddy and Walter. Check out the Wolf and John Lee. Don't forget Buddy. These are the originals." I wasn't an original, but I was glad to be named in that company.

When the British guys like John Mayall, Eric, Beck, Mick, and Keith hit it big over here, they also put their money where their mouth was. When they toured, they had us open for them and told their fans, "These are real cats. Buy their records. Give 'em their dues."

In 1969 the State Department had me go all over East and West Africa. I took my brother Phil along so he might heal quicker from the death of our parents. We had to get eighteen shots before we took off, and I was a little nervous about what I'd find. I knew Africa was nothing like the Tarzan movies I'd seen as a kid, but what would it be like?

Every country was different. Many were primitive, with topless women washing their clothes in a ditch. Other places were more modern. The Peace Corps people were there to escort us. We ate in the homes of diplomats. When our driver wasn't invited in to eat with us, though, I got mad. Inside the diplomat had air conditioning, while outside it was 120 degrees. I told the diplomat I couldn't sit down at his table knowing that the driver was about to have a heat stroke. The diplomat was black, but I could see that he looked down on the driver because the driver's skin wasn't black enough. His skin was lighter. Interesting to see that certain black-on-black prejudices in Africa were opposite ours. For way too long African Americans saw light as better. In Africa I heard some say dark is better. None of it makes sense. It ain't better or worse; it's just different. All prejudice is fucked up.

I met Idi Amin, who requested that I play. Naturally, I did. I didn't know it, but around this same time he was cutting off people's heads. I played best as I could, but later I thought, *Man, what if I had hit the wrong notes?*

Someone asked me when I got back to Chicago if going to Africa felt like going home.

"No," I said. It opened my eyes to a lot of things. I thought I knew poor before, but African poor was on a deeper level. Of course I related to people with skin the color of mine. And I heard music and saw dancing that was new to me but also very old. I felt Africa deep in my soul. But it wasn't my home. Sure, it was the original home, but my real home was Louisiana. Nothing would ever change that.

A few weeks after I was back in the States I ran into B. B. at O'Hare Airport. Both our planes were late, so we had time for coffee.

"We ships passing in the night, ain't we, B?"

"Helluva thing, Buddy," he said. "I'm just lucky to keep working."

"Man, you always gonna be working. You B. B. King."

"The real truth is that I was just about to lose my audience—what with black folks making money, going middle class, and not wanting to hear no blues."

"That audience is just about gone, B."

"Sure is. But here we are playing to a bigger audience that's white and don't have none of their parents' prejudices."

"It's a beautiful thing," I agreed.

"Wasn't for these English acts, I'd be playing a bar in Three Mule, Mississippi. Here I am on my way to Fillmore East in New York City. I think Bill Graham got me booked with the Byrds. Where you off to, Buddy?"

"A traveling hippie festival in Canada. We going by train to four or five different cities. They say it's gonna be bigger than Woodstock."

"Hendrix on it?"

"Don't think so," I said. "But Janis Joplin is."

"You ain't fixing to mess with any of those hippie girls, are you, Buddy?"

"Only every chance I get."

I flew into Toronto, where they had the Festival Express, a custom train just for the musicians on the tour. First gig was Toronto. Then we was riding the rails to Winnipeg and Calgary. These were big outdoor venues for tens of thousands of people. They were calling it Woodstock on Wheels.

I had my brother Phil in my band then, and we had a blast. The other artists were the Band, the Grateful Dead, the Flying Burrito Brothers, Tom Rush, and Ian and Sylvia and the Great Speckled Bird. Janis was the headliner.

I got good respect from the other artists. Janis couldn't have been sweeter. In the high cotton of Hippieland, she was the queen, but she never had no airs about her. But you couldn't separate her from her bottle of Southern Comfort. She clung to it like a baby clinging to a bottle of milk. Janis was flying high. We was all flying high. There were so many drugs on that train that it's a wonder the thing didn't go off the track and float up into the sky. Man, the drugs had exploded. Funny thing about the hippies, though, is that when they smoked up all their dope, they'd come to us for our whiskey and wine. But that was okay with me. Love was in the air, and who don't love love?

This was just a month after the Kent State shootings, so political fever was running high. The concerts had so many kids wanting to get in that they started crashin' down the gates. There were riots. The promoters were going crazy. The fans were saying that the $10 ticket price—a lot for those days—was too high and music should be free. I didn't get paid too much, but I didn't care because this whole new audience was digging what I was doing. The musicians, meanwhile, were complaining that the Canadian Scotch wasn't no stronger than 56 proof. And all the time cameras were rolling. They made a documentary movie of the tour, *Festival Express*.

I loved the tour because of the good vibes with the artists and fans. I wasn't blowing grass, but I got a contact high just being on the train and standing on stage under a heavy cloud of marijuana smoke.

Jerry Garcia came up to me before a show and said, "Buddy you take a hit off this and you'll play some shit you never heard."

I took the hit.

After the show Jerry asked, "Well?"

"You were right," I said. "I didn't hear shit."

Pot ain't my thing.

Couple months later—this is still 1970—the Stones had me and Junior open up their tour in Europe. We went to Finland and France, where the venues were even bigger than Festival Express. I'm talking about soccer stadiums. Mick and Keith were cool—they was always saying nice things about me and Junior. But not all the fans felt like Mick and Keith.

Opening some of them shows, we were booed. Fans wanted the Stones, not two blues cats from Chicago. They'd paid good money to hear their Stones, and I couldn't blame them for being pissed. If I was a hippie living in Helsinki who saved up my hard-earned cash to hear the Rolling Stones, I might be pissed too. I actually felt bad for those people booing. Wish I could have given them what they wanted.

In some cases Junior and I were able to do that. There were some blues lovers out there. When I met them afterward, they told me straight-up that they discovered the blues through the Stones. During those magazine and TV interviews when Keith had mentioned Muddy, the fans went back to listen to Muddy for themselves. It was like B. B. said: the British boys were bringing us along on their ride.

Far as the Stones themselves go, this was the summer after their winter concert at Altamont Speedway in California where there had been a killing. I know that the Stones like to party, but far as I could tell, they were low key on this tour.

It was during this same September that the news came in from London about Jimi Hendrix. He was dead at twenty-seven. Month later the news came in from L.A. that Janis Joplin was also dead and also at twenty-seven.

These deaths broke my heart. Wasn't that I was close to either of them. But our paths had crossed, and I could see their talent and the promise of beautiful careers. Jimi busted through boundaries that needed to come down. Others had come before—I'm thinking of spacey players like Ike Turner, Earl Hooker, and, especially, Johnny Guitar Watson—but Jimi had the balls to carry it into new territory. He wasn't afraid of taking his guitar to the top of a mountain of Marshall amps. He'd turn up the volume loud enough to wake up your grandmother in the grave. That's what he wanted to hear. And he knew that's what the kids wanted to hear.

Janis had her own idols—Tina Turner and Etta James, for sure. She'd be the first to tell you that her mamas were all black. She sang black. She proved that the color of your skin don't have shit to do with the depths of your soul. Janis had soul, but like Jimi, she was a shooting star, quick to shine and quick to flame out.

Sad.

During that same tour with the Stones I got a beautiful surprise. I was backstage at the Paris concert when Eric Clapton came up to me with a funny-looking cat with the face of a foreign diplomat.

"This is Ahmet Ertegun," Eric said, "president of Atlantic Records."

I shook Ertegun's hand, and right away he started saying how much he knew about the blues. He knew a lot. He'd recorded everyone from Ruth Brown to Ray Charles to Solomon Burke to Wilson Pickett. They was all on Atlantic. Atlantic was red hot.

"Ahmet had been chasing after me in America," said Eric, "but I told him he was chasing the wrong man. He should be chasing you."

"Heard you tonight, Buddy, and you were sensational," said Ahmet. "I want to do a real blues album on Atlantic with you and Junior. Good as *Hoodoo Man Blues* was, we want you to surpass it."

"Ahmet's really committed," said Eric. "He's actually going to coproduce it with me. What do you say?"

"I say great. I'm ready. So is Junior. Just say when and where."

"Next month in Florida," said Eric. "I've been working at Atlantic's Criterion Studio in Miami with my Derek and the Dominoes stuff."

Turned out that Eric's Derek band would have a big hit—"Layla"—but that wouldn't come out for a couple more years. Neither would our Atlantic record. It almost didn't come out at all.

Eric is a beautiful man and loyal friend, and recently he told me that while we were cutting the record that came to be known as *Buddy Guy and Junior Wells Play the Blues,* he was wasted bad on drugs and drink. Far as Ahmet went, he spent the days at the beach. We hardly saw him at the studio at all. No one was in charge of nothing. Dr. John came in to play keyboards—and Dr. John's always great—but when he saw what was happening, he said, "Y'all are moving in five different directions at the same time. Plus, the best shit you're playing is happening between the takes, and no one's recording it."

When I complained to Ahmet, he said, "Buddy, don't worry, baby. You cut this record in Miami, and we'll do the next one in Muscle Shoals. I can get you hits in Muscle Shoals."

Hearing that, naturally I got excited. When I thought of Muscle Shoals, I thought of Wilson Pickett hits, Aretha Franklin hits, and Percy Sledge hits. I wanted to record in Muscle Shoals in the worst way, so I stopped complaining about the crazy chaos in the studio and muddled my way through.

There was nothing outstanding about what Junior and me did in Miami. The tunes were predictable, the charts were lame, and the whole operation was a wasted chance to make a mark on a big-time label.

Wouldn't you know that coming out of Florida I'd run into B. B. again. "Oh man," I said, "they playing your song every five minutes." I was talking about "The Thrill Is Gone."

"I never had a hit like this, Buddy."

"'Three O'clock Blues' was big, B," I said.

"Big with blacks. But they playing this 'Thrill' thing on the white stations. They playing it on the same stations where you hear Glen Campbell and the Carpenters."

"I'm happy for you."

"You got a record coming out, Buddy? Seems like the times are right for you."

"Recorded one down in Miami, but it's more a mess than a record. They holding it back. They say they gotta put some sweetening on it."

"Who was the producer?"

"That was the problem, B. No one knew."

"Well, I'm sure something good will come out of it."

I'm not sure something ever did.

It was 1972 before the record came out. On the cover they put the saddest picture of me and Junior they could find. Sad picture, sad record. It sold poorly, Ahmet Ertegun never made good on his promise to send me to Muscle Shoals, and it'd be ten more years before I'd get another shot with a major label.

Rough roads ahead. But hell, wasn't no rougher than what I seen in Toronto one night.

I was up there for a gig, fixing to go on stage before a college crowd when the promoter took me aside and said, "There's a man who wants to sit in with you tonight. You don't have to if you don't wanna, but I thought I'd just ask. His friends are eager to give him some exposure, but he's too shy to ask himself."

"What's his name?"

"You probably haven't heard of him, but he was popular a long time ago."

"What's he called?"

"Lonnie Johnson."

Shock waves went through me. "The Lonnie Johnson who sang 'Tomorrow Night?'"

"Can't tell you. I don't know his songs."

About then I glanced over and saw this distinguished white-haired gentleman holding a guitar. I recognized him from his picture. I went right over and said, "Mr. Lonnie Johnson, it's an honor."

"Thank you, sir."

"Man, there wasn't a time when I wasn't in love with your guitar and your voice."

"I didn't know whether you knew me."

"Everyone knows Lonnie Johnson. B. B. King talks about you all the time. It's a privilege to perform with you. You sing what you want and I'll follow along."

I did just that. Lonnie had to be seventy at the time, but he sang and played like a young man. Listening to the sweetness of his sound and the gentleness of his soul, I had tears running down my face.

Afterward I asked him if he was still living in his hometown, New Orleans.

"Oh, no, Buddy," he said without bitterness. "No one in Louisiana remembers me. Been living up here in Canada, where some fine folks have been caring for me. I've been lucky that way."

I didn't see it that way. Other great entertainers at the end of their careers got to enjoy comfort and fame. Bing Crosby didn't need no charity. Gene Autry got rich enough to buy a baseball team. No one had to run a benefit for Perry Como. Yet here was someone—a bluesman who wasn't just good but was goddamn great, an artist whose spirit inspired dozens of other great artists, a musician who deserved the respect of presidents and kings. Yet when Lonnie Johnson died a few months after I got to play with him, you had to look in the back of the paper to see any little mention of him. Most papers didn't mention him at all.

One thing to live with the blues. Other thing to die with them.

Jailhouse Blues

I been in jail a bunch of times—but never for nothing I did. Went to get Junior out.

It got so bad that one time the cop—a man I knew well—came into where I was playing and put the handcuffs on me.

"What I do?" I asked.

"It ain't for what you did. It's for who you know."

"You can't arrest me for who I know."

"I ain't arresting you—just making sure you don't get away."

We went outside, where he put me in the squad car.

"Who's this about?" I asked, knowing the answer.

"Your brother."

"I was playing with my brother Phil up in the club when you came to get me."

"Not your blood brother," said the cop, "your soul brother."

"If you talkin' 'bout that crazy motherfucker Junior Wells, I ain't responsible for what he did."

"He says you responsible for everything he did. Besides, ain't no one gonna bail him out except you. And we don't want him. We tired of him."

"What do I gotta do to get him out?"

"Give me two hundred and fifty dollars and I give you the pink release papers."

Oh Lord, I thought to myself, *here we go again.*

I forked over the cash. By the time we arrived at the station, I had the papers that would let me take Junior home. I went down to the cell where they was holding him. Man, it smelled like a whiskey sill. Junior was inside, cuddled up in a corner, snoring like he didn't have a problem in the world.

Man guarding him was a brother who must have weighed 350 pounds. He was playing with a chain that held a key.

"Brother," I said. "I came to get Junior."

"You got papers?"

"I do."

"They pink?"

"Pink as pussy."

"Now I need to see something green," he said.

"I already gave the man two hundred fifty dollars."

"So it won't mean nothing for you to give me fifteen."

I reached in my pocket and found only five.

"My last five," I said. "Five's got to be good enough."

"I'll take your five, but you go in that cell and get me another ten. I know your man's gotta be holding ten."

"What if he ain't holding shit?"

"Then you sleep next to him in the cell."

"You gonna lock me in there?"

"One way or the other, I'm gonna get me my fifteen dollars."

"Hold on, good brother," I said. "You best come in here with me. I don't want you out there and me inside. I ain't gonna be locked up with this man."

Guard chuckled, but I still wouldn't step foot in that cell until he was by my side.

We went in together—I was still nervous about the cell door locking behind me—and I right away started poking and shouting at Junior.

"Junior!" I screamed. "Wake up, man, you gotta give me ten dollars so I can pay this man."

Coming out of some dream or nightmare, Junior mumbled, "I ain't giving you nothing."

"I paid two hundred fifty dollars to get you out of here," I said.

"Well, go get your money so we can buy us some drinks."

Even the big bad guard had to laugh at that. At the same time, that didn't stop him from making me search Junior, who, it turned out, had about two dollars in change. The guard took it all and I took Junior home.

The thing that made the bumpy ride with Junior Wells worthwhile was the music. Even though we never made big money as a team and even though no one could never convince Junior that he wasn't gonna replace James Brown, our chemistry was nothing they could make in a science lab. I believe it was magical.

We argued like a married couple. He wasn't a guitarist and I was no harmonica player, but we could both sing. I loved his singing more than I did my own, and I let him sing all he wanted. After all, he'd been in Muddy's band and I hadn't. He had seniority. But in my mind that didn't mean I should shoulder more of the costs.

For example, I bought our first band van. When I'd run it into the ground, I figured it was time for him to buy the next one. He refused. So I refused to play. So he changed his mind and bought the van, but then he started drinking more. When he passed out cold from too much whiskey or wine, I'd snap his picture and put it up in the club where he could see it. He didn't care. When the doctor told him he couldn't smoke due to his punctured lung, I hid his cigarettes. "Don't matter," he said. "Next break I'll run out and buy another pack." And that's just what he did.

After *Hoodoo Man Blues,* I'd say the next best record I did with Junior was *Buddy and the Juniors*. That came through Michael Cuscuna, a music producer.

We were talking one day in Philadelphia when I happened to say, "You know, Michael, when I go on stage with those rock cats and their Marshall amps piled up high as a mountain, they got a volume you can hear from here to Alabama."

"Do you like that, Buddy?" he asked.

"I like it. I've always liked loud, but sometimes it gets to where you can't feel nothing but the loud. You ain't feeling your soul."

"Would you be willing to make a record that went the other way?"

"What you mean?"

"I mean," said Michael, "an acoustic record. No bass player, no drummer—say, just you and Junior and maybe a piano player."

"Who you got in mind?"

"How about a jazz piano player like Junior Mance? That way we could call it *Buddy and the Juniors*."

I had to laugh. And I had to say that I thought it was a good idea.

"If you can pull it off," I told Michael, "I'm there."

Michael pulled it off. Me and the Juniors met in New York City.

We started off playing some of the more famous blues like "Hoochie Coochie Man" and "Five Long Years." Junior Wells was in fine form, and Junior Mance was right on time. With no electricity anywhere, it felt great to hear all those empty spaces around me. I could breathe real good and easy.

Things got so good and easy that when Junior Mance was sitting up in the control booth, me and Junior Wells began making up shit on the spot. Those songs—"Talkin' 'bout Women Obviously," "A Motif Is Just a Riff," and "Buddy's Blues"—were caught on tape and became part of the final album put out by Blue Thumb Records.

By 1971, at age thirty-five, in addition to my girls with Phyllis, I was the father of three other girls—Charlotte, Carlise, Colleen—and three boys—George, Gregory, and Geoffrey—all with Joan. We was living in the two-flat on the South Side. Because I was on the road so much, the marriage was hurting bad. I provided but not nearly in the style that Joan wanted. She wanted more—and I could understand it. The kids wanted more time with me—and I could understand that too. When I got off the road, I was tired. When I played in the city, I didn't get home till the wee hours of the morning. Joan and the kids was living in one world and I was in another.

One incident still burns into my brain. Happened after I had bought a cherry-red El Dorado with a white canvas top. I looked at the Caddie like a beautiful woman—curvy and sexy as hell. Couldn't wait to get in it and drive. Everyone who knew me saw me riding in my El Dorado, proud as I could be.

Well, one night, a month or so after I'd bought the car, I was up in the bed asleep when something told me to open my eyes. I woke up just in time to keep my wife from stabbing me with a letter opener. I got it away from her, so no harm was done, but of course I had to know why she was crazy mad.

"I don't need to tell you," she said. "You can tell me."

"I would if I could," I said. "But I can't. I honestly don't know."

"Bullshit. You got guilt written all over your face."

She stormed out, and I still didn't know. For a week she gave me the cold shoulder. Wouldn't say a word. Finally, we got into it.

"Last Tuesday," she said, "two different girlfriends of mine saw you in Hyde Park riding 'round with some white woman."

"Not me they didn't."

"You got a cherry-red El Dorado with a white canvas top?"

"You know I do."

"Well, a black man in a car that exact model and color was all over this white woman in Hyde Park."

"Wasn't me."

"I don't believe you."

"You don't have to."

"How can you prove it wasn't you?" she asked.

"How can you prove it was?"

"You playing with me."

About then our daughter Charlotte, who was eleven, spoke up. "Last Tuesday Daddy came home early and went to sleep. I remember 'cause I was doing my homework."

"When I drove by the house I didn't see his car," said Joan.

"That's 'cause he parked it out back in the garage," said Charlotte. "He said he didn't want no one knowing he was home so he wouldn't be disturbed."

Joan wanted to double-check, so she went looking for that car. She discovered that Caddie—the one just like mine—in Hyde Park. She realized I was telling the truth. I waited for the apology.

I'm still waiting.

I don't want to sound like I'm saying I was perfect in our marriage—not nearly. On the road I fell to female temptation. But whatever I did, I tried to be discreet—I would never embarrass or humiliate the mother of my children.

When it became clear, though, that our relationship was in the dumpster, I found my pleasures elsewhere. I went through a period when I enjoyed many women. I played around. Turned out, though, running around wasn't my style. Might be fun for a while, but I wanted to settle back down. After Joan and I divorced I was on the lookout for a wife. I guess I always remembered the happiness of Mama and Daddy. That's the kind of trust and love I wanted with a woman.

I also wanted something else—a blues club of my own.

Checkerboard

Not long ago a friend said to me, "Buddy, I know why you had to have your own blues club."

"Why's that?" I asked. I knew, but I wanted to see if he knew.

"Because that's your church, man. That's where you first got religion when you came to Chicago. You got baptized in these funky blues clubs, you got born again, and you can't forget it. When you got worried to see all these churches disappearing, you had to get one for yourself."

That wasn't the answer I expected, but damn if it didn't make sense. I guess I did see the Chicago blues club as something sacred to my heart. Sure, there was drinking and shooting, but it gave me a beautiful feeling like nothing else. It brought a spirit that got all over my soul—and that's something I never wanted to lose.

In 1972 I was thinking that if I had my own club, I might get off the road more. I'd be able to be closer to my kids and, if I played my cards right, might make some money.

I bought the Checkerboard, at 423 East 43rd Street, at a time when prices were low. That's because the hood was going down. Far as I was concerned, though, the hood was always going down. I figured good blues would draw drinkers. Besides that, Pepper's, one of the most famous clubs, had closed down. I hated that the South Side wouldn't have no blues. On the bright side I figured that, what with my work at the F&J in Gary and the club I managed in Joliet, I had good experience. But man, did I have a lot to learn!

Before I opened up a cat said to me, "Buddy, I got only one piece of advice: get a rollaway bed, a gun, and sleep by the register."

I got the gun, but—at least at first—I didn't get the rollaway bed.

First year I got robbed so much that I put up security gates. But the motherfuckers just screwed 'em off and got in anyway. Cost me a hundred to put the gates back up. Then the thieves came back and removed 'em like they was nothing. It was costing me more to put up the gates than what the robbers took.

That's what got me to put up a sign that said, "Don't break the front gate. Go around back. The door's open there. Take what you want."

Of course, I was in the back, waiting for them with a gun. But wouldn't you know that's when they stopped breaking in.

I was selling beer for 35 cents and serving open whiskey only. That meant I'd buy the booze by the half-gallon and pour shots. Thieves couldn't resell open bottles. They were looking to steal whiskey by the case. I learned to keep the stockroom empty.

Folks thought my famous friends would play the Checkerboard and make me a mint. Didn't work that way. For example, the most famous thing that happened at the club, with our capacity of sixty-five, was when the Stones came to film and play with Muddy. They blocked the whole street, keeping out the regular customers, while the Stones's huge entourage of cameramen, engineers, security guards, and friends filled up the place. It was beautiful to see Muddy and the Stones jamming together—turned out to be one of the last things Muddy did—but I didn't hear my cash register ring once.

The Checkerboard was a spiritual blessing but a financial burden. I never broke even and had to use the money I made on the road to keep the doors open. No matter what, I kept the doors open because, as the seventies got disco crazy, the life of the blues was on the line.

Mud in the Burbs

Had to be around 1973 when I went to visit Muddy in Westmont, way out there in the white suburbs, some twenty miles outside the city. He had bought himself a house—nothing fancy, but clean and neat with a little swimming pool in back.

Muddy had been through a lot of changes, the worst being the recent death of his wife Geneva to the cancer. Her passing shook him and, in a strange way, freed him. The Mud had a lot of children from different women, and with Geneva's passing, he got to move them all into his house. He got to be the daddy and granddaddy that he always wanted to be. Wasn't that he didn't love Geneva—he loved the woman with all his heart—but his love life had kept him running this way and that.

When I first came to his house, it was winter. Because it wasn't baseball season, the TV wasn't on. On doctor's orders, the Mud had switched from hard liquor to champagne, and on that day we shared a bottle.

He was happy to see me and asked how things were going at the Checkerboard.

"Going slow, Muddy," I said. "But I ain't quitting."

"Hey, man," he said, "I thought of quitting after *Electric Mud,* but I didn't."

Muddy was talking about the album he'd done with Marshall Chess that brought him a good piece of the hippie market.

"I thought *Electric Mud* sold a ton of records," I said.

"It did. But that psychedelic shit drove me up a wall. Worst part was when I got to the show, they wanted me to play it live—and I couldn't. What's the point of making a record when you can't even play it with your own band?"

"But you liked that thing you did with Mike Bloomfield and Paul Butterfield, didn't you?" I asked, talking about *Fathers and Sons,* a record I loved.

"Oh, yeah," he said. "That was a more natural thing. Those really are my sons. I raised them boys. After that, though, the shit storm hit hard. Leonard sold Chess."

"They say he got ten million dollars."

"Whatever he got, I didn't get a nickel."

"And then Leonard up and died," I said.

"Heart attack—went just like that."

"How old was Leonard, Muddy?"

"Young man, early fifties."

"Is Phil treating you any better?" I asked. Phil was Leonard's brother. "I get little checks now and then. Enough to pay the bills and move me out here."

Couldn't have been much more than a week after that Leonard died that Muddy and his band were in a terrible car accident in Illinois. Three people were killed, including Muddy's driver. Muddy escaped with his life, but his ribs and pelvis got broken, and his hips and back got smashed up. He had surgery that took hours, and he couldn't leave the hospital for months. When he did, he came out walking with a cane. Muddy being Muddy, he picked up his guitar and went back to work. After the *London Howlin' Wolf Sessions* started to sell—that's the record Wolf cut with Clapton, Steve Winwood, Bill Wyman, and Charlie Watts—Chess had Muddy fly to London to do the same kind of thing. I remember Muddy saying, "Those English rock-and-roll cats can play, but they look at me like I done created the world in seven days. They sitting around waiting to see what I wanna play. 'You tell me what *you* motherfuckers wanna play,' I said. 'Let's just play and get paid.'"

That was a couple of years ago. Now Muddy, grieving for the loss of Geneva, was still looking to get paid. We all were.

"Think you'll like it out here?" I asked. "Think you're ever gonna miss the old neighborhood?"

"I can ride down there whenever I want. Besides, you're taking care of it, ain't you?"

"Who's taking care of your old house on South Lake Park?"

"I rented it to Big Eyes."

Big Eyes was Willie Smith, one of Muddy's drummers.

"So you holding on to it, Muddy," I said.

"I figure I best. If I can't pay the note on this motherfucker out here, I can always move back."

Not too long after seeing Muddy I got to catch up with the Wolf. That happened because of the Rolling Stones. They was coming to Chicago for one of their big concerts and sent a limo for me and the Wolf. The plan was to come to their hotel room and then to the show. I was always glad to see Keith and them, but I was especially happy to see the Wolf. Been some time since I'd run into him. At this point he was in his mid-sixties and feeling his age. He'd taken a couple of bad heart attacks. Like Muddy, he'd been in a bad car wreck. His kidneys were fucked up until he was on dialysis. He was walking with a cane, but don't you know he was talking shit just like he always did. And just like I always did, I listened to him like a little child listening to his daddy.

"Did I tell you what happened to me coming outta St. Louis the other month?" Wolf asked me.

"Don't think so."

"Detroit Junior, he was driving my car, and he was pissed at me about something. So he pulls over and is all set to pull me out and whup my ass 'cause he knows I'm old and tired. But what he don't know is that I know I'm old and tired. That's why I don't ever let go of my gun. When he opens the door, he sees my gun before he sees my eyes. 'Whose ass you gonna whip now?' I say. 'Oh, I was just playing, Wolf.' 'Well, I'm playing too,' I say. It's colder than a motherfucker—gotta be below zero—and I think he needs to cool off. 'Best way for you to cool off, Detroit Junior,' I say, 'is to take off your shoes and socks and stand in that cold grass for about forty-five minutes.' 'I can't do that,' he says. 'Well, I *can* blow off your fuckin' head,' I say. I keep my gun on him for forty-five minutes, and for forty-five minutes I'm feeling mighty good about old age."

The Wolf had me laughing.

"If you think that's funny," he said, "lemme tell you about that bass player of yours."

"Jack Myers?"

"That's right. I used him for some college gig up in New York. He wasn't used to playing with me, and I swear he was outta tune."

"Not Jack," I said. "Jack's never outta tune."

"Maybe not outta tune for Buddy Guy, but sure as hell outta tune for Howlin' Wolf. Anyway, the gig's over and we driving back, and I say stop so I can buy me some whiskey. I get my pint and I tell Jack and Hubert Sumlin—'cause Hubert wasn't playing right that night either—I say, 'If you motherfuckers want a drink, don't look at me. The way you was playing was so downright awful that you don't deserve nothing. I even start rhymin' on their asses, saying, 'I just played a college where the students have some knowledge, but I'm having me a fit 'cause my band ain't playing shit.' They start laughing, and I don't like that. I don't like to be laughed at. I say, 'If you ever play outta tune like you did tonight and I don't kick your ass, then Jesus is possum.'"

Wolf is through telling his story just as we arrive at the fancy hotel where the Stones are staying. We get the best whiskey and all the food we want. We shoot the shit for a while and then go to the show, where we're ushered into special seats.

From the stage the Stones say something nice about the Wolf, and that warms my heart because he deserves all the praise in the world. When they introduce him to the crowd, though, I can see the pain in his eyes from how much it hurts to stand. The Wolf was once a powerful man. There was a time when no one in this right mind would fuck with the Wolf. Now the Wolf is old and feeble. Not many of the thousands of people who have come to yell for the Stones bother to look up at the Wolf. They don't really care. But the Stones care. The Stones was the ones who told some American TV shows that they wouldn't go on if Muddy Waters wasn't on there with them. The Stones was good to Muddy and the Wolf, and that's the memory I keep in my heart.

At the end of 1975 me and Junior Wells went on a goodwill State Department trip to the Central African Republic. On Thanksgiving Day it was a hundred degrees with humidity off the chart. We decided to wash our underwear and hang 'em out to dry. After they dried we got dressed and headed out. During the gig that night Junior started complaining about a terrible pain in his butt. We went to a doctor who right away knew what happened.

"You did one of two things," he told Junior. "You either sat on a wet toilet seat or you hung out your underwear to dry."

"Yes, sir," Junior said, "I hung out my underwear."

"That's when the moisture got a fly to lay an egg. And the egg hatched a worm. And the worm got in your backside."

"Ouch!" I said.

"How you gonna get it out?" asked Junior.

Doctor picked up a tool that looked like a can opener.

"Oh Lord," said Junior.

"It's quick," said the doctor, "and it'll do the trick."

After the doctor got the worm out of Junior I said, "One thing's for sure—from now on, wherever I am in Africa, I'm gonna shit like a cow standing in the meadow. I ain't sitting on no toilet seat. And I ain't washing out no underwear."

While we were there I asked the doctor to check my blood pressure. I'd been taking medicine because it was too high.

Blood pressure was okay, but the doctor asked, "Let me see your blood pressure pills."

He looked 'em over and said, "Hope you haven't been looking for any women over here."

"Why do you say that?" I asked.

"Because with this blood pressure medicine, you ain't got no nature."

"My doctor didn't tell me that."

"When you get home, ask him."

"I will."

And I did. And sure enough, he had forgotten to mention that. I had him adjust the dosage so my nature come back.

It was the first week of January in 1976 when we arrived back at O'Hare. The heat in Africa was unbearable, but the snow in

Chicago was piled up high. Minutes after we landed we heard the news.

"The Wolf is dead," someone said. "The cancer killed him."

Junior knew him for a longer time than I did. "There ain't ever gonna be another Wolf," he said.

That was the truth. I remembered something else that was true, something that Hubert Sumlin said about the Wolf. He meant it with love and respect when he said, "Wolf ain't no natural man. He's a beast."

"You think of those cats like Charley Patton and Robert Johnson," Junior said as we drove from the airport into the city. "We didn't get to play with them. But we was blessed to play with the Wolf."

All I could say was "Amen."

Sixty-Three

The Wolf made sixty-five. When I think of how hard he lived, I'm amazed he made it that long. When he died, I couldn't help but think how much I loved these men who were my teachers, fathers, and friends. I had to be the luckiest guy alive to take that train on September 25, 1957, and get to Chicago when these beautiful guys were still going strong. They breathed their blues all over the city, all over the musicians—first the black ones and then the white ones, and then musicians far away as Africa and Asia.

By the middle of the seventies the company that bought Chess got bought by someone else who closed down the studio.

"I was on that label for nearly thirty years," Muddy said. "They keep calling it Chess, but it ain't Chess. The real Chess died with Leonard."

"Who you gonna record for?" I asked.

"Ain't sure and ain't worried, 'cause someone will have me."

April of 1976 the phone rang.

"Buddy Guy," said the man with a Southern accent. "This is Clifford Antone. I have a club down in Austin, and I'm your biggest fan."

"Well, thank you, sir," I said. "Never felt too welcome down there in Texas." I told him the story about my time in Texas with Elmore James and the club owner who put the gun to Elmore's head.

"This is a different deal, Buddy," said Clifford. "This is my club. And I want to bring you and Junior Wells down to surprise Muddy for his sixty-third birthday party. Gonna send you both first-class tickets and put you up in a first-class hotel. You won't have to play but a few numbers."

"I'll play all night if you wanna."

Clifford didn't talk like an owner. He talked like a fan. He talked about how he brought Eddie Taylor back together with Jimmy Reed. He talked about a group of white boys called the Fabulous Thunderbirds with a guitarist named Jimmie Vaughan and a harp man called Kim Wilson. He said how much Muddy loved them and promised I would too.

When me and Junior arrived in Austin, Clifford was there to take us around. Turned out he was from Port Arthur, Janis Joplin's hometown. He told us how his people were from Lebanon and got into the grocery business. The man treated us like kings. I remember him saying, "Having you guys here is like having the president and the pope on the same stage."

The club was at Sixth Street and Brazos. Clifford said he was building it as a monument to the blues.

While Muddy was performing we snuck backstage so he wouldn't see us. As I was listening Clifford said, "Those are the Fabulous Thunderbirds. That's the Jimmie Vaughan I was telling you about."

The thing between Jimmie and his harp man reminded me of the thing between Muddy and Little Walter—it was right tight. Jimmie didn't play with no gimmicks. He played blues the way blues should be played. He knew what not to play and how to make you wanna hear more.

When it was time to sing "Happy Birthday," me and Junior came waltzing out on stage with the cake. You could've knocked the Mud over with a feather. He was grinning from ear to ear. He told the audience, "See these here boys? I known 'em since they was kids. I raised 'em."

We all got into playing "Got My Mojo Working" real strong, and I got to feeling that, even in this age of disco, maybe blues could still draw a crowd. Seemed like the public had turned their back on the blues, but down here in Texas they was blues crazy. And this man Clifford Antone had a love for the music as powerful as anyone I've ever met. I was thinking—no, I was *feeling*—that love might be reason enough to go to sleep that night with a little hope in my heart.

Another Texan named Johnny Winter helped Muddy by producing an album on Columbia Records.

"After all these many years, felt strange cutting a record for someone other than Chess," said Muddy, "but it also felt good. Johnny knew how to work me."

"You use Winter's band?" I asked.

"Plus Pinetop on piano, Big Eyes on drums, and Cotton on harp."

Muddy sounded excited about it. I went back to his house for a visit and was glad to see him in good health and high spirits.

"What you calling the record?"

He laughed before saying, "When we got through, I could feel my dick getting hard. So I'm calling it *Hard Again*. What do you think?"

"I think Muddy Waters is ready go out there and chase down some more nineteen-year-olds."

I was glad Muddy was finding new success, but I was going nowhere fast. I wasn't gigging all that much out of town. In town I played at the Checkerboard where business wasn't booming. I was hanging on—wasn't about to give up on my blues club—but this was a time, late in the seventies, when the blues got a bad case of the blues.

I remember being at a blues festival when I overheard two fans talking. They didn't know my face, so they was free to say what they believed. They was looking over the program when one cat said to the other, "Buddy Guy is on the bill. You know who he is?"

"One of those old blues guys."

"How old?"

"Buddy Guy? Oh man, he's been around. Got to be in his nineties."

At the time I was forty-three.

I couldn't get the attention of any of the major record labels. Even the minor ones wouldn't come my way. I was in France when a local man called Didier Tricard said he'd record me and my brother Phil. Cat let us do anything we wanted, and I have to say that *Stone Crazy*—where I got to be me—still sounds pretty goddamn good. Didier said he would even let me name the label he'd issue it on. I called it Isabell for my mom. We cut it in Toulouse and got to play loose and free. No one really heard the record, though, and it got lost in the shuffle.

Same kind of story with a cat from England, John Stedman. He came over and recorded me and Phil live at the Checkerboard in 1979. He caught some good jams and put out the record on his JSP label, but it didn't make no noise. Far as the American labels went, Buddy Guy was stale as last week's moldy bread.

The thing with Junior was also hurting bad. His drinking was making him do and say things that, when sober, he'd never say or do. When he played poker, he started wearing a holster that held two guns. If he won and got happy—or if he lost and got unhappy—he'd start into shooting holes in the wall. That would bring out the police, who'd haul him off to jail and come get me for the bail.

We'd still get called out to California for gigs, but the money was so small that we'd have to use pickup bands that had a hard time following us. I'd try to whip the cats into shape, but Junior—not the world's most patient man—would go off and threaten the lives of any musician who messed up his time.

In Boston I left my motel room to get some ice when I happened to glance down the hallway at the Coke machine. There was Junior, naked as the day he was born.

"Go in and put on some clothes," I said.

"Why?" he asked.

"'Cause I don't want them to kick us outta here."

"Why would they do that?"

"Ever hear of indecent exposure?"

"Ain't nothing indecent 'bout being naked. Women like seeing me naked. One's up in my room who's buck naked herself. She's fixing to come down here and join me."

"Oh Lord" was all I could say.

Junior was losing it. He was even losing it on stage with me. If he thought I was playing too long or too loud, he'd grab the neck of my guitar to stop me. His big number, of course, was "Messin' with the Kid." That was his showpiece. I liked playing it. Didn't even mind playing it twice on the same night. But when one night he demanded we play it six straight times, I had to say, "Junior, I ain't messin' with that kid no more."

I told you how Muddy would beat on a woman—well, Junior, bless his heart, would get beat *by* a woman. A couple of them hurt him pretty bad. Once a singer down in Austin, Lou Ann Barton, a white girl who worked with the Vaughan brothers and sang the blues black, had Junior chasing her all over the club, whispering, "Pussy, pussy, pussy" in her ear. She wanted to be left alone, and when Junior wouldn't stop messin' with her, she hauled off and socked him in the jaw. He collapsed like a house of cards.

Because of his drinking, our shows kept getting shorter. Got harder for him to stand up there and perform for very long. I couldn't have that. I've never missed a gig for fear of disappointing fans. And when I saw that look of disappointment on the fans' faces because our shows were so short, I felt terrible. I wanted to stay up there and keep the show going on my own, but Junior wouldn't have it.

By the end of the seventies I couldn't have him anymore. If I wanted to keep him as a brother and friend, I knew I'd have to end our professional relationship. It wasn't easy. Not only did I love the man, I also loved his music. We were a couple married in the blood of the blues. In the minds of many fans we belonged together. And on a business level we had drawing power.

People warned me against cutting him off. One cat said, "You need him to get those bookings. They don't want Buddy Guy. They want Buddy Guy and Junior Wells."

"He's been half-stepping," I said. "He ain't all there."

"Half of Junior is better than no Junior at all."

"I've always done things on my own. I'll be fine."

"You'll be broke."

"I'm already broke."

"You'll be broker."

No use arguing. The aggravation wasn't worth whatever extra bookings I'd get with Junior on the bill. By the start of a new decade—the eighties—Junior and I were traveling down different roads. Once in a while we'd bump into each other. He was always welcome at the Checkerboard, but we was never a team again.

Weeds Keep Growing

I was born into agriculture. Growing things interests me. There's a sure-enough science to cultivate the earth in a way that gets you what you want. Seeds are amazing. You plant 'em, you water 'em, you watch for the results. You gotta deal with nature in a way that respects nature's own program. Go against nature, and nature will fuck you.

Sometimes, though, nature will spring a surprise on your ass. Nature will up and say, "Here's some weeds that are gonna grow no matter what you do. Try to kill 'em and they'll come back strong. You can trim 'em, but you can't get rid of 'em. They stronger than whatever chemical and poisons you wanna spray over 'em. They connected to the earth."

The blues is like one of them weeds. The blues is rooted so deep into the ground, spreading so far and growing so fast, that nothing can stop 'em. For a year or two or three you might think they gone. You might think that other kinds of music have drowned them out. But one day you'll be looking out your window and you'll see 'em everywhere—a whole backyard of blues. Not only that, they running over your neighbors' yard and all over the neighborhood. They everywhere.

I say that because the blues, due to the English rock and rollers, came back in the sixties only to back off in the seventies. But then in the eighties the blues got born again, this time stronger than ever.

They got born again because they too good to stay dead. They too simple, too pretty, too true to real life. When you break down all the guitar music starting up with the rock and roll of the fifties, you see the blues at the root of the whole thing. Can't ever get away from the blues. Your mama might have passed on, but she'll always be your mama. Long as you live, you ain't ever forgetting her. She gave you life. Well, sir, the blues is life.

In the eighties my life was a slow build. Back in '75, Jennifer became my second wife. She was a fine woman who seemed to understand me. She renewed my hopes for a happy life. We had two wonderful children, Rashawnna and Michael. The marriage wasn't perfect, but it lasted more than thirty years, and that's saying something.

In the eighties I also started hearing about younger black bluesmen like Robert Cray. Robert was great. He had a rock audience and he was selling records. Clifford Antone in Austin proved to be one of my angels. He kept bringing me down there to play. I got close to Jimmie Vaughan and then Jimmie's kid brother, Stevie Ray.

Stevie was the one who really led the kids back to the blues. His Double Trouble started tearing it up all over the world. Was just three guys—Stevie, Tommy Shannon on bass, and Chris Layton on drums—but man, they had a big sound. Stevie talked about me and Albert Collins like I talked about Muddy and the Wolf. He respected his elders. Him and his brother came from Dallas where, as kids, they heard Freddie King. They grew up on the true blues. Jimmie was more traditional than Stevie, who was deep into Jimi

Hendrix. To my ears Stevie had a way of combining Jimi and Albert King that created something new.

I say it was new—because he played with young fire and young feeling—but it was also old. Stevie was a student. He knew every last blues guitarist who came before him. But Stevie wasn't afraid of bringing attention to himself. He reminded me of how I was when I first got to Chicago. I'd do anything to get attention—that was Stevie.

Talkin' 'bout Albert King, he was something else. Unlike me, he had him some big hits back in the sixties like "Born under a Bad Sign." Along with Otis Redding, Booker T., and the MGs, Albert was a star on Stax Records, where he got famous for playing that Gibson Flying V. He was also big as a bear and could be twice as mean. Albert stung them strings hard, and ain't no doubt that he was one of the best. Fixed up a stinging style all his own. I'm just glad I didn't have to work for him.

We was at the North Sea Jazz Festival, where I was scheduled to go on before him. I wanted to holler at Albert, just to say hello, but when I started to knock on the door to his dressing room, the security guys came running over like I was about to disturb the King of Norway.

"You can't knock on that door," one of the cats said. "Mr. King don't allow it."

"I'm an old friend," I said.

"He give you permission?"

"I don't need no fuckin' permission," I said, before yelling, "*Albert! You in there?*"

He came out and gave me a big hello. He was smoking his pipe. You never did see Albert King without his pipe.

"Hey, man," I said, "they acting like I was trying to rob you."

"I don't even let my band members back here," he said.

"How come?"

"I gotta let 'em know who's boss."

"You do that when you hand out the check, don't you?"

"Talkin' 'bout checks," said Albert, "they paying us pretty goddamn good at this festival."

"They is. My sidemen are happy."

"You pay 'em more when you get more?" asked Albert.

"Don't you?"

"Fuck no, man. Why should I?"

"Seems only fair."

"What you call fair? It's fair of me to hire these motherfuckers. If they ain't playing with me, they playing with themselves at home or driving a taxicab back in Memphis."

Albert was great, but he was cold.

Muddy was sick. He had the cancer. I knew it and so did a lot of other people. But I also knew Muddy well enough to know that he didn't wanna talk about it. At the same time, I had to go see him. I couldn't stay away.

It was March 1983. I knew that his seventieth birthday was coming up in April. (He said he was gonna be sixty-eight, but we later learned that he'd cut a couple of years off his age.)

"Hey, Muddy," I said, as I walked through the door. "Brought you rice and beans."

"That's good," he said. "Go in the kitchen and heat 'em up."

He was sitting on the couch. As I passed by I saw how thin he'd become. He looked weak and tired. The television was playing an old shoot-'em-up movie.

I heated up the food and brought it to him on a tray.

"You want a beer?" I asked him.

"Thanks, Buddy. Beer would be good."

I went to the fridge, pulled out two beers, popped the tops, and carried them to the living room. I sat on the couch next to Muddy.

"Go ahead and eat," I said. "It'll do you good."

"Man, I know. I got to eat more."

I watched him fool with the food, but he had no appetite. He took one swig of beer and that was it. We just sat there watching the movie.

"I know you're looking forward to April," I said. "Opening Day. How the Sox gonna do?"

Muddy always liked to talk baseball.

"Think we're gonna win it all this year," he said. "Think Carlton Fisk and Rudy Law gonna be strong. Pitching is strong."

"LaMarr Hoyt and Richard Dotson," I said, mentioning two of the White Sox's aces.

"And don't forget my boy Jerry Koosman."

"Well, we'll go to Comiskey Park and I'll let you buy me hot dog."

Muddy nodded his head and gave me a little smile.

Didn't wanna mention music 'cause I knew he wasn't performing or recording. Figured the best thing I could do was just sit and be quiet. Sat there for a long spell.

Muddy was the kinda guy who could read my mind. After a long time he turned to me and said, "Look, Buddy, I'm okay. And I only got one thing to say to you."

"What's that?" I asked.

"Motherfucker," he answered, "don't let these blues die."

A month later, on April 30, the Mud was gone. He made seventy, and he made Opening Day, but he didn't get to see his Sox win their division that year.

The funeral was held 'round the corner from the Checkerboard. We was all torn up until we couldn't talk. All we could do was play.

All the cats were there—James Cotton, Hubert Sumlin, Sunnyland Slim. That night they came to the Checkerboard, and we cried through our guitars, harps, and pianos. We cried when we sang and we sang until we couldn't sing no more. We sang every Muddy song that Muddy ever taught us. We remembered the man whose spirit gave new blues to an old city. He was the one who warmed up ice-cold Chicago with the sun of the Delta. Man, he was the son of the Delta—the source, the father to a thousand musicians, to cats who knew him and cats who weren't even born. He's still giving birth to the children of the blues.

I just love saying his name. I just love telling everyone that Muddy Waters was my friend, that Muddy Waters was the man.

They renamed the street next to his house on the South Side Muddy Waters Drive. But then, years later, there was talking of selling or destroying that same home at 4339 South Lake Park. Thank God I had me enough money so I could buy and preserve it. Now no one's ever gonna tear it down, just like no one's ever gonna forget Muddy.

Alpine Valley

I didn't have no real record deal in the eighties, but thanks to the younger cats like Robert Cray and the Vaughan Brothers, and thanks to Clifford Antone turning Austin into a capital of the blues, I got more gigs. Asia and Europe were calling on a regular basis. The venues were bigger, and the fans demanded repeat performances. It was great, but I can't say it was all good.

One time I was paid good money to open for AC/DC. Their fans, though, weren't my fans. When I got out there, I was smacked with a chorus of loud boos. I felt bad—not for myself but for the people who'd paid to hear heavy metal hard rock, not electric blues. I wanted to tell them that I understood their disappointment, but I kept quiet and played my set, acting like the boos were really cheers.

In 1985, no matter how much I loved my club, the Checkerboard was a drain. It drank up money like a drunk drinking up whiskey. The area was crumbling, and I was tired of using my road money to pay for the losses. Even with all those headaches, I would have stayed except for the landlord pulling some underhanded moves to get rid of me. Because I was the one who kept the blues in the hood, the landlord's attitude got me mad. But rather than fight, I up and left. I promised myself that as soon as I could find a good property, I'd invest in another club.

That happened in 1989, when I was finally making good money gigging over the world. One of the reasons the Checkerboard never turned a profit was 'cause people from the outside got tired of their cars getting stolen when they came to the South Side. I started looking around an up-and-coming neighborhood they was calling the South Loop, just beyond the big stores on Michigan and State but close to the lake. I found me a spot at 754 South Wabash. I liked it because it was near the huge Hilton Hotel where conventioneers stayed year round. Conventioneers like to party on blues. They could walk from the Hilton to my place in just a few minutes. It was bigger and cleaner than the Checkerboard, and I was all set to name it the Dew Drop Inn, after the famous Dew Drop Inn in New Orleans where Guitar Slim played. My lawyer, though, said there were legal problems with that name, so I'd better come up with another. I settled on Legends because I was dedicating the club to all the legends—Muddy, Walter, Wolf, Sonny Boy, John Lee, B. B., and all the others—who had schooled me.

The location proved good, and business was much improved from what I'd been experiencing. It's hard to be too unhappy when you're making money. I was feeling good.

I was feeling even better when Eric invited me over to London for his Prince Albert Hall concerts. That's when I got to be good friends with the great piano man Johnny Johnson.

Johnny was famous for playing with Chuck Berry. He's the Johnny of "Johnny B. Goode." I never met him before, so when I got to my hotel and saw a note from him saying he wanted to have breakfast the next morning, I was excited.

At 8 a.m. I heard a tap on my door. I opened it and saw Johnny.

"You get my note?" he asked.

"I was just fixing to meet you at the breakfast restaurant," I said.

He pointed to an attaché case he was carrying and said, "I got our breakfast right here."

He opened up the case and brought out a bottle of Crown Royal.

"Any objections?" he asked.

"Johnny," I said, "I'm so happy to meet you that I'll go along with any kind of breakfast you want."

As we drank, he started telling me how "Johnny B. Goode" was something he wrote with Chuck. He said he was a writer on almost all of Chuck's hits.

"I came up with the rhythms and the music," he said, "and Chuck wrote the words. Back then I thought whoever wrote the words wrote the song but later came to learn that the music is worth half. Tried to make some kind of deal with Chuck, but Chuck wouldn't talk. 'I wrote, "Roll Over Beethoven," Chuck said to me. 'That was my idea.' 'Yes,' I said to him, 'but that was the only lyrics.' 'The lyrics,' said Chuck, 'sold the song.'"

Took Johnny a while, but he did sue Chuck, though by then too much time had passed and I don't think he got any money. I was able to give him money, though, for appearing at Legends several times. I also got to play with him, and although no one could ever match Otis Spann, when it came to the keys, you didn't wanna fuck with Johnny Johnson.

In August of 1990 Clapton called and said he was coming to Chicago, where him, the Vaughan Brothers, and Robert Cray were playing an outdoor concert in Alpine Valley, a ski resort in Wisconsin eighty miles outside Chicago. I wasn't on the bill, but Eric wanted me to come along to jam.

I knew Eric had given up drinking and drugging a long time before this, and he told me that Stevie and Jimmie had also stopped. Everyone was in great shape. To celebrate I was cooking a giant gumbo at Legends the day after the concert.

On the way to Alpine Valley Eric said to me, "Hey, Buddy, haven't heard a record from you in a while."

"That's 'cause I don't have a deal."

"That's crazy. I've copied all your old licks. How am I going learn your new licks if you don't have a new record?"

I had to laugh.

"I'm going to take you into the studio myself," said Eric.

"Anytime, baby, any place."

When we got to the venue, it was like old homecoming week. Stevie and Jimmie were healthy and happy. Hadn't seen Stevie since July of last year, when he came to Legends to join me on my birthday. Jimmie told me how he'd quit the Fabulous Thunderbirds to make this tour with his baby brother—first time they'd ever toured together. On stage Jimmie would put his arms around Stevie while they played on the same guitar. It was a beautiful thing to see.

Stevie's set was blazing hot. He did everything but jump on his guitar and ride it to the moon. When he played my song "Leave My Girl Alone," he looked at me in the wings and winked. I appreciated that. Never heard Stevie wail so hard. I got goose bumps. I felt proud. Just like Muddy had felt he had raised me, I felt like Stevie was my boy.

"How the hell am I going follow this?" asked Eric, who was standing next to me and waiting to go on.

"All you can do is try," I said.

Eric had no problems. He was the star of the show, and the crowd loved him. I do believe that, pound for pound, Eric Clapton is the most popular man to ever pick up a guitar.

After his set he brought me out, and all of us—Jimmie, Stevie, Robert Cray, and Eric—jammed on "Sweet Home Chicago." Whenever I'm around, Eric always calls that tune. We wore it out, and the fans went home smiling. Backstage, with everyone glowing, Eric talked about how we'd be together again at his concerts at the Royal Alpert Hall in London. He was gonna bring us all in.

To avoid the mess of traffic, helicopters were flying us all back to Chicago. Stevie was eager to get back, so he got the last seat on the first chopper. I went up in one with Eric and Eric's manager. The fog was coming in, and that made me a little uneasy, but I figured that 'cause choppers went straight up, we'd be above the fog in no time. We were.

Landed at Midway, where I said goodnight to Eric and reminded him that I was cooking a gumbo and the whole gang was invited.

"You can't really cook, Buddy, can you?" he asked.

"You'll see for yourself. This thing is gonna be so bad it'll hurt your mouth."

We hugged and went our separate ways.

Went to sleep and, as usual, got up early in the morning. I was off to buy shellfish for the gumbo. It was gonna be an all-day creation.

First call I got was one of my daughters.

"Daddy, daddy!" she was screaming all hysterical. "Are you dead?"

"What you talkin' 'bout, girl? How could I be dead if I'm talking to you?"

"They said you were on a helicopter that crashed last night."

"No helicopter crashed last night."'

"That's not what they're saying on the news."

"What they saying?"

"People were killed."

"Which people?"

"I don't know."

Next call I got came from someone who had the facts.

"Been a terrible accident," he said.

"Everyone alright?"

"No. Stevie's dead."

Stevie's dead. Those words didn't make no sense. I was sure I heard 'em wrong.

"Say again," I said.

"Stevie's dead."

"Stevie Ray Vaughan?"

"The chopper carrying Stevie and three guys from Eric's team backed into the side of a hill after takeoff. Them and the pilot were killed on impact."

I just flopped. I crumbled. I couldn't say or do nothing.

Stevie's dead.

With the rest of the world, I cried for Stevie. He was a shining star that fell out the sky just when his star was on the rise. Wasn't no reason for it except for something my folks always said: "When your time's up, ain't nothing you can do."

Day of his funeral I had booked a big gig with Carlos Santana at Legends. Me and him was playing together, and the place had been sold out for months. I asked Carlos what he wanted to do.

A spiritual cat, Carlos said, "I don't think it's about what I want to do, Buddy. I think it's about what Stevie would want us to do."

"Stevie would want us to play the blues," I said.

And that's what we did, dedicating the night to him. We played our hearts out, but our heads weren't right. When it comes to thinking how we lost Stevie, my head still isn't right.

Wasn't until I played with Eric at Prince Albert Hall that I saw Jimmie again. That was 1991. Was the first time Jimmie played in public since his baby brother had passed. When we jammed together, I think Jimmie was able to grieve the best way a musician knows how. That's when we let the music carry our tears.

After one of the concerts at Prince Albert Hall a man introduced himself to me as Andrew Lauder. Said he was the boss at Silvertone Records. Turned out that Silvertone was in London, but they was owned by Sony. Was I willing to sign with Silvertone?

Was I willing?

Hell, more than willing, I'd been waiting for this chance for years. I guess you'd have to call Chess a major label in the blues, but they never paid nobody major money—and besides, they never knew what to do with me. I did some things for Bob Koester's Delmark, but that was a tiny company. Vanguard was bigger, but they just wanted the Chess sound.

"You can sound any way you wanna, Buddy," said Lauder. "I believe you've been under-recorded and recorded wrong. We want to bring out your fire."

"Let's do it," I said.

"It'll help to bring in a producer."

"Who you got in mind?"

"Do you know John Porter?"

"No."

"Do you know Roxy Music?"

"Just the name, not the music."

"Well, John was their bass player for a while, and then their producer."

"He English?" I said.

"Yes. Does that count against him?"

"No, that counts *for* him. Jimi Hendrix didn't have no hits till he came to England. I'm seeing England as good luck."

"We're seeing you, Buddy, as one of our most important artists."

"I'm seeing you, Andrew," I said, "as a godsend."

John Porter was cool. At the session in London he dropped "Mustang Sally" in my lap, but I didn't mind because it's a strong song and I love me some rhythm and blues. Also loved that John worked hard to let me sound the way I sound live. He also didn't mind me cutting four of my own songs. One of them became real important. Happened 'cause I was trying to shoot pool before the recording session. Cat was joking around when he said to me, "Well, you can't play pool, but can you play the blues?" My answer was "Damn right, I can play the blues." That sparked an idea for a song: "Damn Right, I've Got the Blues." Turned into the album title and the biggest hit of my career.

Jeff Beck dropped by to play on a couple of tracks, and Clapton played on one. The pieces fell into place. If you listen to the album right, what you hear is a man used to wearing handcuffs flying free as a bird. And if you ask me my favorite track, I'll tell you this story:

I wanted to honor Stevie. I thought about playing one of his songs, but that didn't seem right. They was his tunes, not mine. Then I thought about writing a new song for him with words to express my love. But the words wouldn't come. So I decided to do something different. I went to the studio, told them to cut off the lights, and just started playing.

"What are you doing?" the producer asked.

"Rememberin' Stevie," I said.

"Rememberin' Stevie" became the name of the song.

While I was playing, my mind went back to Alpine Valley. That was such a beautiful night. After Stevie came off stage I was sitting in a corner fooling with my guitar while Eric started his set. Stevie came over to listen to what I was doing.

"Buddy," he said, "you slay me with your licks."

"After that what you done played out there you can't stay nothing to me. You slayed everybody. I'm still recovering."

"Know what, Buddy? We got to make a record. We got to do something together."

"I'm ready, Stevie. I been ready."

"It's gonna happen. It's got to."

Rememberin' Stevie, I thought that if it did happen, it was gonna happen in blues heaven. I pictured the band—Muddy Waters, Otis Spann, Fred Below, Little Walter, Stevie Ray Vaughan. That's a band worth dying for.

Hoodoo Men

If an artist tells you he don't care nothing about prizes, chances are he's lying. I'm not saying that making the music isn't the important thing—it is. That's the real pleasure. And I'm not saying that pleasing people ain't also important—I always wanna do that. But there's another kind of recognition that feels good: being called up to the stage for one of them Grammys is a thrill like nothing else. It happened to me at age fifty-five when I won a 1991 Grammy for *Damn Right, I've Got the Blues.* Thank you, Jesus.

Over the next twenty years, I'd win five more Grammys. I started getting a slew of recognition—*Billboard* magazine's Century Award, membership into the Rock and Roll Hall of Fame, the Blues Foundation's Keeping the Blues Alive Award. Every one of them was wonderful. Don't take nothing for granted. But when these prizes came in, I felt like they really belonged to Guitar Slim or Lightnin' Slim or Lightnin' Hopkins—the cats who came before me and never got the right fame or the right money.

I was finally in the position I wanted: getting a good advance from an international music company that let me cut my kind of record. I also got fatter fees on the road. That let me invest more money back into my club until I finally moved it down the street and bought the building where it's now housed at 700 South Wabash. I can't say I'm at the top of the ladder, but I've moved up a lot of rungs since those days when no major label wanted to look at me.

These records on Silvertone, coming out so regularly, helped keep me in the public eye. Over the years Eric came back to play on some of my records—along with B. B., Carlos Santana, Keith Richards, Jonny Lang, Derek Trucks, Susan Tedeschi, Tracy Chapman, and John Mayer. All the different generations helped me out, and we blended together real natural.

I had great producers—John Porter, Eddie Kramer, Steve Jordan, David Z, Dennis Hering, Tom Hambridge. They knew to give me the fun and freedom I needed. Also glad that these records are all different, especially the one called *Sweet Tea* that I made around my sixty-fifth birthday. That let me go to Oxford, Mississippi, to Dennis Hering's studio and record the acoustic feeling of the old guys I love so well. I played songs by Junior Kimbrough, who'd made beautiful albums on the Fat Possum label. I never did meet Junior—he passed in 1998—but the style he built in North Mississippi was something I felt deeply. Him and cats like James "T-Model" Ford wrote like the men I heard as a boy—the men sitting on the porch, making quiet magic with their guitars, and singing the sun to sleep behind those white and gold fields of cotton and corn.

If you want to understand friendship among men, listen to the last thing I did with Junior Wells. Silvertone put it out in 1998, the year Junior died. It's called *Last Time Around—Live at Legends*.

Hadn't played with Junior in six or seven years. So much water had passed under the bridge. There had been hurt feelings on both sides. I had my issues, and God knows, he had his. But I'll be damned if playing with him still wasn't the best feeling a man could have. Between us, the blues was a blood bond. Didn't matter none what had been said in the past. We sang and played in the present, and that night we fell in love all over again.

I liked that our last session was stripped down. The music was naked, mainly my acoustic guitar and Junior's harp, my voice and his. What I liked best was when we went back to visit "Hoodoo Man Blues," the song that made the world see us as a team.

Maybe you'll be thinking I'm bragging, but I do believe that the Buddy-Junior team will go down in the history of the blues as a combination that worked real well. He brought out my funk. I like to think that I brought out his. When he sang over what I played, tears rolled down my cheeks.

Tears rolled down my cheeks when I went to Junior's funeral. The cancer had gotten to him like it had gotten to Muddy. He was tired and frail at the end. He was ready to go home. That day we put him to rest, I looked around and saw certain females from his life that I thought should be laying out in that coffin instead of him. But I didn't say nothin'. I just thought good thoughts about the man who left behind a musical treasure. Wrong or right, he lived his blues. He *was* the blues. My brother.

Three years later, in 2001, another one of my daddies died. Talkin' 'bout the great John Lee Hooker. Got to say that it was one of the wonders of my life that a man whose "Boogie Chillen" got me started as a child turned out to be a friend. When I think of Johnny and his way of walking through the world, I got to laugh. I look at him like a tribal chief, a guru, and a sacred spirit.

Back in the seventies Marvin Gaye put out an album called *Let's Get It On.* I loved it, but then again I loved everything Marvin put out. At the end of the record he sang this song called "Just to Keep You Satisfied." Talking to his lady, he says something like, "I put up with your all your jealousy and bitching too, but I forget it all once in bed with you." He's telling his wife goodbye and feeling terrible about how he couldn't give her what she wanted. He keeps saying that it's too late to save the thing. Man, I related.

That's what happened with my first wife, Joan, and my second wife, Jennifer. I tried, but I failed. Both times I was a-wishing that this was the relationship to stay steady till the end. I don't like drama. Don't like arguments and split-ups, don't like to see tears, and don't like to feel no heartaches. But the heartaches came, and so did the split-ups.

My kids suffered. They suffered because their mothers and me couldn't keep it together, and they suffered because I was out there on the road. Now they all grown up, and I have me a crew of grandkids, and I've been able, best as I can, to make up for lost time. Me and my kids are together a lot. We talk, we laugh, and they don't mind when I fix 'em dinner. They know the old man can cook.

In recent years I lost my dear brother Phil, my bandmate and best friend for so many good years. Miss Phil every day.

Lately I been out there sharing dates with B. B. King. That's a privilege. We get to talk about the days of picking and plowing. Just being in his company makes me shout with joy. B. B. played on my last record, *Living Proof*, on a song called "Stay Around a Little Longer." We was singing to each other.

Another song on that album was "74 Years Young." Now I'm seventy-five. My health is good. My fingers still work. My voice has held out. My fans haven't left me. They accept what I offer and give back plenty love.

What else can a man want?

Good beans, good corn, fresh fruit, fish that ain't polluted, pork that ain't spoiled, and chicken without none of them crazy growth hormones.

If you see me walking up and down the aisle of the supermarket, you'll know what I'm looking for. Food not pumped up with poisons and chemicals. Food that makes me think of Mama and Daddy and how they saw us through. It's not that I think good food's gonna let me live forever; it's just that good food, like good blues, makes life better. It ain't phony. It comes from nature. It nourishes and satisfies your hunger for something real.

So let me tell you goodbye the same way I said hello.

Let me invite you to Legends.

If you come by my club in Chicago, you probably won't notice me sitting at the bar. Most people don't. That's okay. I'm happy to enjoy the music along with everyone else.

But if it's a slow night at the counter where we sell my merchandise, I'll get on stage to sing a song. That lets people know that I'm in the house and available to sign T-shirts, CDs, and my trademark guitars. I never mind drumming up business.

I also never mind thinking back on this long journey that keeps getting longer. I think about that train ride from Louisiana to Illinois on September 25, 1957, and the blues I found when I got to Chicago. Like me, that blues left home. The blues went traveling and wound up in every corner of the world.

I'm believing that the blues makes life better wherever it goes—and I'll tell you why: even when the blues is sad, it turns your sadness to joy. And ain't that a beautiful thing?

Selected Discography

The Sixties

On Cobra:

The Cobra Records Story (Capricorn)

On Chess:

Folk Singer (with Muddy Waters)

Buddy's Blues (Chess 50th Anniversary Collection)

"Wang Dang Doodle" (from Koko Taylor: *What It Takes, The Chess Years*)

On Delmark:

Hoodoo Man Blues (with Junior Wells)

On Vanguard:

A Man and the Blues

On Universal:

"The Motor City Is Burning" (from *The Definitive Collection: John Lee Hooker*)

The Seventies

On Hip-O Select:

Buddy and the Juniors

On Alligator:

Stone Crazy

The Eighties

On JSP:

D.J. Play My Blues
Breaking Out

The Nineties

On Silvertone:

Damn Right, I've Got the Blues
Last Time Around: Live at Legends (with Junior Wells)

2000 and Beyond

On Silvertone:

Sweet Tea
Skin Deep
Living Proof

Acknowledgments

Buddy Guy Would Like to Thank

This book would not have been possible if it were not for the love of my family, the support of my friends, the hard work of my staff, and the unwavering dedication of my fans across the world. I am eternally grateful to everyone who has come into my life and played a role, whether that role has been great or small. You have all inspired me.

First, I would like to thank David Ritz for translating my life into this incredible story. Thank you to Vigliano Associates for believing in this project that is so close to my heart.

I would like to thank my family. My parents, Sam and Isabell Guy. My mother always worried about me, as I was her only child to leave Baton Rouge, so to keep a smile on her face, I promised her that I was going to Chicago to work and one day I would come back home in a polka dot Cadillac. Even though she never got to see me play, my polka dot guitar will always be a symbol of the promise that I made to her. Thank you to my siblings, Annie Mae, Fannie Mae, Sam, and Philip. Thank you to my children, Charlotte and son-in-law Mark Nunn, Carlise, Nanette, George Jr., Gregory, Geoffrey, Shawnna, Michael, and all of my grandchildren. I love you all.

I would like to thank my dear friends Junior Wells, Uncle Harry (aka "Babe"), Jack, and Homie for their unconditional friendship over the years. Although Junior, Babe, and Jack are no longer with us, they will never be forgotten.

Thank you to my producer, Tom Hambridge, who continues to be a source of inspiration before, during, and after the recording process.

To my band and crew, Tim Austin, Gilbert Garza, Ric Hall, Marty Sammon, Philip Vaandrager, and Orlando Wright. I couldn't be more grateful for your dedication and hard work.

I also want to thank Annie Lawlor, Isabelle Libmann, and Michael Maxson of GBG Artist Management for always keeping me on track. Thank you to Brian Fadden, Myrna Gates, Michael Greco, Harvey McCarter, Johnny Sims, and the entire staff of Buddy Guy's Legends. Thank you for making Legends the greatest blues club in the world. Also, to our patrons—from our local regulars to those who come from around the world, I would like to thank each of you for continuing to support Legends for over twenty-two years. Your patronage means everything to me.

I would like to thank Michael Tedesco, Dan Mackta, and all of the folks at Silvertone Records; Garry Buck, Ron Kaplan, Paul Goldman, and the staff of Monterey International; Maureen McGuire and the folks at MacCabe & McGuire; Paul Natkin, Chuck Lanza, and Tom Marker. Your collective hard work is appreciated so much more than you will ever know.

Thank you to the city of Chicago for all your support in helping me keep the Blues alive. Thank you to New Roads (Pointe Coupe Parish), Louisiana for bestowing such an amazing gift upon me, for it is a blessing to receive such an honor.

Finally, I would like to thank all of the blues men who came before me who never received the recognition that was due to them. They were the red carpet that rolled out for us to walk up. When I went looking for their sound, there was no textbook to help me. I had to find the notes myself. I may not have found them, but I found something else along the way. For that, I thank you from the bottom of my heart. If I have failed to mention anyone, please forgive my mind and not my heart, for I am truly grateful to you all.

David Ritz Would Like to Thank

Buddy Guy, for honoring me with this collaboration.

Ben Schafer—great editor, great guy—Jimmie Wood—great pal, great guitarist—David Vigliano, David Peak, Ruth Ondarza, Harry

Weinger, Herb Powell, Lou Ann Burton, Alan Eisenstock, John Tayloe, John Bryant, James Austin, Dejon Mayes, Dave Stein, Aaron Cohen, Juan Moscoso, Ian Valentine, Dennis Franklin, and Skip Smith.

Special gratitude to my dear friend Jimmie Vaughan, who many years ago said, "Why don't you write Buddy Guy's book?"

Endless love to my family, my beautiful bride, Roberta; wonderful daughters, Ali and Jess; wonderful grandkids, Charlotte, Nins, James, and Isaac; sisters Elizabeth and Esther; nieces and nephews; sons-in-love, Henry and Jim.

Thanks to the men's groups from Tuesday and Saturday mornings.

I call my savior Jesus and love calling his holy name.

Index